Sunrise by Christine, at 12

Legacy of Laughter

A GRANDPARENT GUIDE AND PLAYBOOK

Mary Kay Morrison

Photography by Don Morrison

Enjoy
Mary Kay

Humor Quest

Caledonia, Illinois

Published by Humor Quest
322 Canary Drive Caledonia, IL 61011

ISBN: 978-1-7367913-0-1
Library of Congress Control Number: 2021907881

Credits:

Editor and Production Designer:
Deborah McKew, *Words in Play*

Cover Artist and Graphics: Kyle Edgell

Additional Graphic Design: John Kitchen, Linda Mirabile

Special thanks to the Association for Applied and Therapeutic Humor, an international nonprofit organization of professionals who study, practice, and promote healthy humor. www.aath.org

Contributors

Grandchildren: Co-authors and Artists
(in birth order)

Ben Heinisch
Tyler Heinisch
Andrew Heinisch
Samuel Heinisch
Emma Heinisch
Maria (Mimi) Heinisch
Christine Heinisch
Katie Van Heuklon
Steve Heinisch
Cloe Van Heuklon
Isaiah Heinisch
Faith Heinisch

Children's quotes are identified by the name of the grandchild and their age when they wrote it. The spelling (including errors) is often taken directly from their journals.

Immediate Family:

Don Morrison, Husband
William Heinisch/Jennifer Heinisch
Andy Heinisch/Julie Heinisch
Rachael Van Heuklon/Jason Van Heuklon
Peter Heinisch/Valerie Heinisch

Family and Friends:

Ros Ben-Moshe,
Barb Best
Jan Bowman
Karyn Buxman
Brenda Elsagher
Deb Gauldin
Ray Heinisch
Jan/Bob Jakeway
Jill Knox
Kathy Laurenhue
Bev Letcher
Chip Lutz
Katherine Puckett
Joyce Saltman
Jean Smith
Amy Wasil

This book is dedicated to my soulmate and incredible husband Don,

to our amazing children and their spouses,

to our awesome grandchildren who were the inspiration and collaborators for this book:

Ben
Tyler
Andrew
Samuel
Emma
Mimi
Christine
Katie
Steve
Cloe
Isaiah
Faith

and to grandparents who are making a difference every day!

In memory of . . .

My parents, Bill and Ruth Wiltz

My dear friend, Jill Knox, who listened patiently to my initial ideas and encouraged me during the challenging times as well as contributed several quotes for this book. I am grateful for the opportunity to have been her friend and colleague for many years. Her life was a blessing for all who knew her and I will always be grateful for her friendship.

Colleagues Peter Jonas and Kay Caskey who shared their insights and testimonials for my work.

What the Experts are Saying about Legacy of Laughter

This book will contribute to your personal well being. It raises the meaning in life component by making you aware that it is in your hands what legacy you want to leave. How you want to be remembered by your grandchildren is actually a very effective positive intervention generated within positive psychology. Writing a letter from a grandchild that remembers you and what you mean to them make people aware what good they can still do in their remaining time. Invokinging humor and playfulness will also enhance two further elements of well being, namely positive emotions, and positive relationships. So, in addition to being interesting and very insightful ,you can also regard Legacy of Laughter: A Grandparent Guide and Playbook as useful remedy, but I will see my copy as sheer fun to read.

"...sheer fun to read."

—Willibald Ruch, Ph.D., University of Zurich
Department of Psychology, Personality and Assessment

Mary Kay Morrison has done it again! Based on the neuroscience of learning, this book provides grandparents, or any caregiver, with valid information, and a sense of relief as the reader sees that everyone makes mistakes! Any adverse childhood experiences that your grandchild may have can be balanced by positive experiences; you will find ideas for many in the grandparent Playbook. Social Emotional Learning and the Brain research tells us that it only takes one caring adult to impact a child's life. In some households the parents are that supportive person, in others, it's grandparents. As a grandparent who closely follows the educational neuroscience research, I choose to be that caring adult whenever one of my grandchildren need me.

"Based on the neuroscience of learning, this book provides grandparents, or any caregiver, with valid information, and a sense of relief as the reader sees that everyone makes mistakes!"

Mary Kay refers to the term "outlaws" in this book as she talks about the "other" grandparents and relatives. Choose to be the "real" grandparent, the one the grandkids know will show up for events in a flash. Taking into consideration that we can't all be there ALL the time, Mary Kay provides ideas about communicating from a distance—a must in our present climate!

Whether it's your first-time grand parenting or you feel like you are a pro, this book will provide you with useful ideas. The situations and anecdotes are laced with humor, Morrison's specialty.

—Marilee Sprenger

The grandkids are coming over and I look at my pathetic basket of old toys and books and realize that I can do better! I only have two grandkids, not like this author with her 12 "grands," but I do want to be a fantastic grandmother. While reading Legacy of Laughter, I was amazed at not only her creative ideas, but how she was able to personalize them for each grandchild. I vacillated between, "Geez, who is this woman and when does she sleep?" to being so very thankful that someone took the time to not only give me ideas on how to best serve my grandchildren and their parents, but to add the humor that comes from looking at life on the lighter side.

"...you will find it helpful and hilarious."

Mary Kay's philosophies, along with anecdotes of her own parents, demonstrate many ways to share with grandchildren. An observer of human nature, the author has a way of explaining not only how to go about creating magical moments, but she relates how it helps them developmentally. This book gives me more confidence to put these ideas into action.

She has a grandparent survival kit to be prepared for any occasion. For example, a Tootsie roll sucker, not for the kids—for the grand parents to chomp on when their own children leave them a 20-page letter of instructions on how to care for their children.

As an educator, she highlights the power of imagination by including poems and quotes from her grandchildren. I love the way she mixes the ideas, the stories of the families and grandchildren, along with a lighthearted explanation of why it's so important to have relationships with your "grands." Although I know I can't follow every strategy in this book, it inspires me to be a better grandparent and put my own dreams and ambitions into it. This is a great blend of a how-to book, an affirmation guide, and practical explanations. It gave me guidance as a new grandmother, with a healthy dose of good humor. I am sure you will find it helpful and hilarious.

—Brenda Elsagher, CSP
National Speaker, Author and Comedian

Few people have the knowledge that Mary Kay has on what humor and play can do for you and, even if they do, it's more talk than action. Mary Kay's playful knowledge turns into playful action in every aspect of her life. She doesn't just talk it, she jumps ropes to it. This is especially evident with the way she is with her grandkids. From making cookies to creating special paths for each of them in her woods, it's all fun and that fun is a legacy that will live with them their entire lives. (I wish she were my grandma!)

—Chip Lutz, MS, MA, CSP, CHP

Mary Kay Morrison delights in cartwheeling toward a joyous life. Her much anticipated book combines research-based findings with her own and her grandchildren's practical experiences. Grandparents will savour this treasure trove of practical suggestions for play.

—Kathy Klaus, Social Worker, Entrepreneur, Toy Designer and Author, *Wild Ride*

Mary Kay Morrison inspired me to be the best " Bubbe" (Yiddish for Grandma) BEFORE I even became a grandparent. I witnessed firsthand how she organized her play and craft room, and how she and her husband made special walking paths (on their land) for each grandchild. Mary Kay knows the science and psychology of creating memories for the future and the importance of being present in play. I am grateful for her grandparent wisdom.

—Deb Hart: ≠–Humorist & Author, Speaker, Officiate, Spiritual and Grief Support

As What to Expect When You're Expecting became my favorite reference when I anticipated parenthood, Legacy of Laughter is my "go-to" source as a creative and playful grandparent. I enjoyed a close relationship with my grandmothers, but now I strive for an even tighter bond with my grandchildren, especially because they live far away. My time with them in person is so precious, as is the time on the phone and online via FaceTime and Zoom. As a former nurse educator and fellow member of AATH, I know the value of laughter in adult learning. But Mary Kay's book empowers me to bring joyful play to a whole new level with my beloved grandchildren. Her wise advice and the insights shared by her own grandchildren inspire me to try new ways of incorporating humor and laughter into our conversations and our play. I love that she bravely shared her "bloopers" so that I truly laugh and learn from her missteps. The "Legacy of Laughter" is this grandma's favorite grandparenting bible.

—Deb Price, RN, MSN
Science Writer/Editor, IQ Solutions: Author: *Love's Last Act*

It started the day I saw the 12 toothbrushes, each identified by the name of the grandchild. Then I noticed the 12 craft bins for each child. I casually mentioned that Mary Kay should write another book—this time about ideas for grandparents! Mary Kay has a wealth of creativity, ingenuity, and ideas to share with all of us grandparents. There is so much more to this book beyond toothbrushes and craft bins. It's a book I will treasure and revisit numerous times!

—Kathy Brown, High School Friend and Inspiration for this book.

This book will provide some happiness and fun in these difficult times of Covid-19.

—Don and Alleen Nilsen, Professors Emeriti A.S.U. Emeritus College, Co-Founders: International Society for Humor Studies

"A great gift for any new grandparent!"

This is such a wonderful book. Lots of great suggestions, ideas and welcome advice from a pro. True sage, concrete advice you can't get anywhere else, such as: "Make sure you release captured insects from the Tupperware container before the next grandchild visit." Mary Kay walks her talk. I have been to her basement/playground. A true paradise for children of all ages. This is a great gift for any new grandparent!

—Laurie Young

In Memory of Peter Jonas who passed away after he wrote this for the book:

It takes a lot of courage, strength, and naps to be a grandparent. And it takes even more intelligence and extraordinary effort to make it fun. But leave it to author Mary Kay Morrison to be able to write about the experience of grandparenting in a fun, easy to read, and practical manner. Mary Kay not only delivers emotional and enduring stories, but she does it in style, using such expressions as: "On becoming a humor being," developing a "playbook for pun fun," and demonstrating the "Superpower of grandparents." This book is great fun and dare I say, a practical guide on establishing treasured traditions with grandkids. Like Mary Kay, I have read thousands of books to my grandkids, and taken just as many naps, but this book is just what every grandparent needs.

—Peter M. Jonas, PhD
College Professor, Consultant, and Proud grandparent

Bubbles were one of my favorite thing to do for fun. I would use them to help with my little cousins who would love to blow bubbles with me.

Mimi, at 16

Contents

Preface

While there are extraordinary benefits to digital technology, there is also unprecedented concern about the impact that this technology is having on kids. Children as young as two have become hooked on devices. Some are experiencing an addiction to screen time that is actually impacting their physical and mental health. The world-wide pandemic has magnified these challenges when education via zoom becomes the selected option for learning. Medical experts agree that the lack of exercise and reduced amount of time for play is negatively impacting kid's cognitive development.

Grandparents have a unique opportunity to secure, enhance and apply their superpowers to make a significant difference in the lives of their grandchildren. A loving relationship that involves playful interactions will provide incredible benefits for their grandchildren and may even convince kids to spend more time developing their playful intelligence (Anthony DeBenedet, *Playful Intelligence*).

The research on the benefits of humor and laughter is quite clear. We know that laughter can reduce stress and maximize learning. Play is the key ingredient in promoting brain growth. It is a powerful trigger for laughter. My mission has been to not only promote the benefits of play for children, but to change the prevalent ageism mindset that play is just for kids. Humor and laughter are key ingredients for healthy aging. Play is beneficial for kids and for their grandparents. The spice of humor and a playful attitude can improve the ability to laugh during life challenges.

I invite you to join me and share the laughter! When we laugh, our grandkids catch it! Laughter is contagious! Infect your grandchildren. I guarantee laughter and play will support their ability to not only survive in their digital world, but to thrive.

Note: Many of the information in this book is based on my previous two book publications, *Using Humor To Maximize Learning* and *Using Humor to Maximize Living*.

Foreword

by Rachael Van Heuklon

As a young girl, I remember looking into the stands of my gymnastics meets and seeing the face of a person that immediately made me feel at ease, loved, and supported. Over the years and hundreds of sporting events, drama performances, and music concerts later, the support continued, not only for myself and siblings, but my own children and all the other grandchildren. This is my loving, caring, goofy, funny, and supportive mom.

Even though there are twelve grandchildren, she has the gift of making each one feel valued, loved, and a special part of the family. She has a unique relationship with each one while giving their parents comic relief and support in the joys and challenges of raising kids.

Mom has always been a fun parent and grandma with multiple activities including gingerbread- house building, monster pancake/cookie baking, pogo stick jumping contests, museum visits, painting lessons, bug and toad collecting helper, and flower gardening expert. The list could go on and on.

She has always encouraged play, laughter, and resilience in her relationships with her kids and grandchildren. This book will provide so many useful ideas in fostering those fun relationships in the grandparenting adventure!

The author and her daughter Rachael.

It is always fun to have some of my family come
to cheer for me at my volleyball games.

Emma, at 15
Artwork by Emma, at 6

Footprints from Past to Future Generations

The announcement came unexpectedly at Thanksgiving dinner, when I asked my son, William, if he would like another piece of pie. He immediately responded, "No, but Jennifer would …she's eating for three!" Everyone all started simultaneously laughing and crying with delight at this news.

WOW! We were going to be grandparents of twins!

The rush of feelings—from amazement to overwhelming joy—were interspersed with flashbacks on the quick passage of time. It seemed like just yesterday when my first son was born. As I relived that sweet memory, I experienced overwhelming gratitude for my own parents who had been quite active and engaged in our children's lives. My mom Ruth Duncan Wiltz was there when each of my four babies arrived. She mended torn blankies and always arrived at our house with delicious pies or angel food cake.

My father Bill Wiltz absolutely delighted in playing with his grandkids. He taught them card games including the Wiltz family game of 7-Up. His love of nature was contagious, and the kids were amazed at his ability to imitate the call of a cardinal. His sense of fun, silly jokes, and laughter will long be remembered. Over the years, we were able to celebrate many holidays and family events with my parents. My father would have thoroughly enjoyed his great grandchildren, but he died of early onset Alzheimer's disease before they were born. It is a treasured memory that my mom was able to welcome and hold each of our 12 grandbabies. My parents' unwavering love and support flashed through my mind after William made this announcement.

Wow! I was going to be "A GRANDMA!"

I wondered what this grandparenting thing would look like? The media had fed my stereotyped grandparent image of gray hair, boxy black shoes, and granny glasses. I always assumed I would be "old" when I had a grandchild.

But I did not feel old.

I want to live forever in the hearts of my grandchildren.

Advice for New Grandparents:

Keep your mouth shut and follow the rules.

Brenda Elsagher
author, speaker, educator, friend

I knew that I wanted to have an energetic and active relationship with these precious little ones. I wanted to share my sense of fun and laughter. As I processed this glorious news, the flashbacks of extraordinary moments caressing my first baby were interspersed with the anxieties that I had experienced as a new parent.

Grandparents understand the dynamic mix of ecstasy and uncertainties experienced by new parents, and I instinctively knew my son and his wife would be incredible parents. I also realized that having twins probably meant little or no sleep for them for the first few months. I found myself thinking, "Oh my gosh—they have no idea of what they are getting into." I somehow had the good sense not to say that out loud, as we joyfully celebrated their news. Unconditional parental support would continue in this new role.

As I was visualizing what this new "grandparent" role would be like, I was in the process of writing my first book *Using Humor to Maximize Learning*. My grandparent experience has unquestionably been shaped by my in-depth study on the neuroscience of learning.

Exploring the research on the benefits of play has been a significant factor in developing my grandparenting philosophy. I understood that the inclusion of play and laughter would nurture my grandchildren, but I had no idea how much it would contribute to my own well-being.

Wow! I was going to be "A GRANDMA!"

The Magic of New Beginnings

If I had known grandchildren were so much fun, I'd have had them first!

Get ready for the ride of your life! If being a parent is similar to a roller-coaster ride with countless ups and downs, twists and turns, it is true that the grand ride goes even faster! Grandparenting is a unique opportunity to be immersed in magical moments without the nitty-gritty, everyday parenting distractions of laundry and meal planning. As your children step onto their own parenting journey, let them know you will be there for both the thrills and the bumps.

Over the next few months you will have conversations about delivery, baby names, birth, and childcare. It may be entertaining to share some amusing stories about your own experiences but keep it light. When we went to the hospital at midnight for the birth of our first child, the father rang the emergency bell. He said: "Uh…I have a delivery to make." Stick to funny and positive stories. Do not (I repeat, DO NOT) tell gruesome tales.

Anticipate and respect the golden hour, that first magical hour of attachment between just the parents and that precious new little one. It is their sacred time for bonding.

Artwork by Katie, at 14

When I was in 8th grade, my mom was expecting another baby. We had many discussions about what the name might be. I repeatedly suggested Fabian (the name of my favorite singer at that time.) Fortunately, my mother did not listen to me. Michael is the name of my brother, who was actually named after my great grandfather. Perhaps a boy's name has been passed down for several generations or Rose was a favorite aunt's name. You can make suggestions, but whatever name the parents choose, know that it will soon be a favorite of yours.

Miraculous Moments

Tears flooded my eyes when the tiny hand grasped my outreached finger. I felt gentle power in that serene trust, and I knew this was the beginning of a lifelong bond. Those precious first moments are captured forever in my heart. The nurses in the hospital gave me a "New Grandparent" pin. What a fun way to celebrate!

You will recall that the first few weeks with a newborn are both exhilarating and exhausting. Grandparents are usually eager to plan a home visit as soon as possible. Your relationship with your son or daughter will guide your decisions on those trips. Those first interactions may need to be short and sweet. Offers of meals and help with laundry will be appreciated. Most parents will be grateful for gifts including the practical one of hand sanitizer. Wash your hands and use the sanitizer before you hold that precious newborn!

These identical twin boys have enriched our lives beyond measure. We were blessed that our son and daughter-in-law were happy to have our enthusiastic assistance. We kept the twins overnight a few times in that first month so the parents could get some sleep.

Since both boys seemed to be hungry at the same time, we spent much of the night rocking and feeding them. When they finally went to sleep, I must admit that I heard every quiet sigh and tiny movement. I frequently tiptoed into their bedroom just to be sure they were still breathing, and to once again rejoice in the miracle of their precious birth.

GRANDMA'S HOUSE

Artwork by Christine, at 14

As full-time working parents of twin sons (and four years later, a daughter), life was very hectic!
Our parents/grandparents were so supportive! The support they gave then, and continue to give, is appreciated more than we can ever repay!

Jennifer, daughter-in-law

The 3 Rs

* REMEMBER to limit advice

  "When I had you…" Do not give opinions unless asked! (Confession: I was not always successful at this and remember several times when I wished I had kept my thoughts to myself.)

* RESPECT instructions

  "What do you mean you want me to wake her every two hours to feed her?" Follow parent guidelines—even though you know a better way to do it. Yes, you probably do! Recognize that infant care guidelines have evolved over the years and there are always evolving philosophies on best practice.

* RESTRAIN from bragging too much

  Of course, your grandkids are the cutest kids in the world, but posting 100 pictures a day on social media might be overkill. Be sure the parents are okay with you posting pictures or notes about their children.

The Extended Family

New parents can experience quite a bit of anxiety in striving to meet the expectations of family and friends. Maximize opportunities for positive interactions while respecting the diverse traditions of the other side of the family. Babies bring a whole new perspective to their "village." Shared enthusiasm about the arrival of this baby can generate lasting friendships with an entirely new community of relatives.

"Outlaws" is our affectionate name for
the other sets of grandparents.
Realize you have also become an "outlaw."

We have enjoyed bantering with the outlaws that the world's most beautiful grandchild has been created with a blend of our "amazing" genes. Meeting that wild aunt and/or outrageous cousin will add to the remarkable dynamics of this baby's family circle.

LOL MAGIC

When I found out my daughter was pregnant, I started the "baby library." I sent a book every other week for her to read to her unborn baby. I will continue to send books after she is born, always with an inscription of love.

Jill Knox, friend

WACKY WEDNESDAY
by Dr. Seuss

As you attend events (baptisms, preschool programs, and sporting events), you will have the opportunity to get to know a variety of family members. We have been grateful for these friendships that have been added to our lives.

Some ideas to help enhance family relationships:

* Invite the parents and the extended family to your house for birthday celebrations or special events.

* Make the effort to get to know the outlaws on a personal basis. Find out what interests you might have in common. We enjoyed meeting for lunch, playing games, and attending events together.

* Communicate with them the positive impact their child has had on your family.

When there are several sets of grandparents, make every effort to strive for frequent, positive communication. There may be circumstances of divorce or other difficult situations within families. Put aside any disagreements and make every effort to smile your way through the difficult moments.

We are grateful that these children are blessed with four (or more) grandparents who love them and are willing to cooperate, collaborate, and welcome each other into their families! We celebrate how much each pair of grandparents adds to the family equation and how much we genuinely like one another.

—*Bev Letcher, friend*

No cowboy was ever faster on the draw than a grandparent pulling out their phone to share grandkid pictures.

Order a phone case cover with a grandchild picture for a quick way to brag about your cute and exceedingly smart grandbaby.

I really appreciate mom doing art with the kids. It is a special experience for Samuel and Christine. We are all proud of the work they create. Many are displayed in our house for us to enjoy daily.

Peter, author's son

Art by Christine, at 11

Showers of Support

Baby showers are a good time to get to know the other side of the family. Offer to co-host events and collaborate on the food, decorations, and games.

❋ Gift childhood baby scrapbooks or photo albums.

At one of my first showers, my Aunt Angie gifted her daughter-in-law with my cousin's baby book at their family baby shower. Maureen was delighted to see pictures of Jerry when he was an infant. My children have also appreciated this tradition. It was intriguing to learn about the first smile, and how old they were for their first steps. Infant pictures of the baby's parents add to the delightful anticipation of the newborn's arrival.

❋ Dust off and wrap that framed picture of your child. Include a memorable story with the photo.

❋ Fill a beautiful box with family keepsakes. Birth certificates and other mementoes can be framed for preservation and gifted.

❋ Create a collage of family baby pictures. If possible, include grandparents and great grandparents.

❋ Offer a virtual option for those who cannot attend in person. The shower can also be recorded and shared later.

❋ Hold a baby picture contest. Ask everyone to bring a baby picture in an envelope. Put them on a large poster board and ask people to identify them. Or ask people to email or text their baby pictures and do a slide show so everyone can guess at once.

❋ When my daughter was pregnant, I created a scrapbook of her childhood pictures. These were a powerful reminder of our changing roles, and the continuation of family bonds. I included some philosophical poems and quotes about mothers and daughters. As she was expecting a daughter, it was a reminder of the strength of the women in our family who have contributed to our heritage. We were blessed to share this celebration with my mother who crocheted a beautiful blanket to embrace this great grandchild.

Gift Idea:
Diaper Survival Kit

- hazmat suit
- face mask
- neoprene gloves
- sponge (to mop up the most egregious offenses)
- kitchen tongs (so no handling of the diaper actually has to occur)

Amy Wasil, friend

Great Grandma Ruth Wiltz with Emma and Samuel. Generational photos are a treasure!

A Spirit of Peace

Honor the wishes of the parents in their spiritual choices and celebrate in whatever way they choose. When appropriate, share that special christening gown or other significant item passed down through generations. A gown could be worn for a ceremony or repurposed as a baby pillow or quilt. Emma was our first granddaughter, and I was thrilled that she wore the christening gown that I had worn for my own baptism.

Your heart will frequently be touched by priceless moments. I treasure those extraordinary peaceful flashbacks of wonder that I experienced with each of our twelve precious grandbabies. My antique rocking chair holds extraordinary memories of singing and rocking these sweet babies to sleep. Each grandchild has forever touched our hearts with the magic of their unique spirit.

Just as I want to live forever in their hearts, I know that they will live forever in mine.

Emma, our first granddaughter, wore my christening dress for her baptism. My hope is that she will continue to share the gown as part of a tradition that will reflect her own spiritual journey.

This picture of my mom Ruth Wiltz with our grandchildren is one of those priceless moments that will live forever in my heart.

Just as I want to live
forever in their hearts,
I know that they will live
forever in mine.

Cloe, at 11

Over the three days of summer I spent at Grandma's, I had a great time. I caught the cutest toad that you will ever see. I named him, Toadie. Grandma helped me make him a little habitat container complete with a little toad house, three inches of dirt, moss, and a small bowl of water. I have always wanted a pet toad, and I love Toadie.

Cloe, at 11

Embrace Your Special Sauce

2

Each grandparent will formulate a special recipe for stirring the gift of laughter into interactions with their grandchild. Embrace your special sauce! Grandparents have an extraordinary and unique opportunity to nurture grandkids and to make a significant impact on their life.

In order to maximize your special sauce, let's review the identified benefits of humor to include in your recipe with a perfect blend of ingredients.

The 4 Benefits of Humor

The research on the psychology of humor suggests that there are numerous benefits for infusing humor into difficult situations. The emotional bonds of trust, hope, optimism, and love are the foundation of a laughter-filled relationship (Morrison 2008).

1. *Trust:* Fun and laughter are indicators of a high level of trust within a healthy relationship.

2. *Hope:* Humor is the sign of positivity within individuals and organizations. Humor expresses the hope that we can survive tragedy, difficulty, and change and not only survive, but thrive.

3. *Optimism:* The energy of humor reflects a confident spirit. Humor practice and a focus on positivity can decrease stress and depression.

4. *Love:* When exploring close relationships, the number one characteristic mentioned as vital is a sense of humor. Laughter is a universal connection that builds rapport and supports a loving relationship.

These qualities will be integrated throughout the book as a basis for sharing your own special blend of laughter sauce with your grandchild.

What will your grandchildren

remember about you?

11

Maximize Self Care

Take care of YOU in order to take care of your grandchild! You will want to enjoy the joyful magic of this new journey. Balancing expectations and new challenges can be both exhilarating and exhausting. Your health is an important factor for spending optimal time with your grandchild. Be realistic and optimistic about your energy and capabilities.

❋ Maximize Fitness

If you are not working out, now is a good time to start! You will be able to do more with your grandchild if you are in shape. Simple weightlifting, and a cardio routine are highly recommended. If you are not already working out, get going! **You are not too old, and it is never too late.** Besides, you have a few months, and this is your contribution to the labor.

❋ Maximize Time

Look at your current schedule for any adjustments that you might want to make to include time for childcare opportunities and for travel for long-distance visits.

❋ Maximize Healthy Eating

Enjoy more blueberries, salmon, and chocolate (especially chocolate.) Not only good for you, but a powerful example for your grandchild. Not sure how well I am doing with modeling this. **My teenage grandkids think that trail mix is M&Ms with obstacles.**

❋ Maximize Positivity

Begin a journal and record your grand journey. Look for the humor in everyday life and the ability to see funny! As you get older, you've got to stay positive. For instance, the other day, I fell down the stairs. Instead of getting upset, I thought, "Wow, That's the fastest I've moved in years."

This gives me an extra incentive to take better care of myself.

—Jill Knox, friend
*when she learned she
was to be a grandma*

Take time to smell the flowers.
Painted plaque by Mimi, at 12

Find the Laughter!
I really don't mind getting older,
but my body is taking it badly.

Yvonne Garris

Caregiving Options

Often grandparents are willing and able to offer support with childcare. Parents are often worried about leaving their baby and are usually most comfortable with having grandparents provide childcare.

There are a variety of options for grandparents to become involved:

✳ Regular Child Care

Parents may request this option, so they can return to work knowing their child is getting the best care possible. Some grandparents are happy to be invited to provide everyday childcare. Make sure any arrangements are acceptable to all concerned. It is important to clarify times, location, discipline, philosophies, and compensation options ahead of time.

✳ Back-up Child Care

Many grandparents offer to be the person who will care for their grandchild when there is an emergency, a sick child, or an unexpected change of plans. Again, be sure to clarify the details for arrangements.

✳ Periodic Child Care

New parents find they no longer have the freedom of going to dinner and a movie. Offering childcare for parent date-nights or vacations is appreciated.

One shock that came with providing childcare was getting extremely detailed written instructions. I was certain, that since I was an experienced parent, my children would recognize that I knew the ropes about infant care. I was amazed when they left several pages of detailed, written instructions for care. When leaving the second born there would be a few written notes. For the third child, there might be a few directions called out as they were closing the door behind them.

As their families have grown, we chuckled about the fact the later children not only get fewer pictures taken, but fewer concern about germs and routines.

You never stop being a parent no matter how old your kids get.

—Chip Lutz, friend

Find the Laughter!

First child eats dirt.
Parent calls the doctor.

Second child eats dirt.
Parent cleans out mouth.

Third child eats dirt.
Parent wonders if they need to feed them lunch.

My parents went to the beach and we got to stay at Grandma's

Emma, at 7

During long times apart, I send riddles every day via email. The Subject line says "Monday Riddles from Grandma."

Joyce Saltman, author, speaker, professor, friend

If grandkids are interested in their grandparent's hobbies, progress can be nurtured long distance. When together, grandparents teach the kids and leave them with materials to practice their skills. The kids can show their progress through pictures or Skype.

Rachael, daughter

Smiles Across the Miles

Grandparents who live quite a distance from their family can experience significant anxiety. There are a variety of strategies that can minimize the miles. Some grandparents may even make the decision to move closer. Others get a small apartment or mobile home nearby to make frequent trips easier. Before the birth, begin discussions about how you will "shorten the miles" and how frequently visits can be arranged.

While it is difficult to live a distance from your grandchild, there are many creative ways to shorten the miles and to interact with laughter and love.

City Street by Cloe, at 9

❋ Snail Mail

Include pictures of yourself in letters for the parents to show and hang where your grandbaby will see them. As they get older, include small amusing gifts. Stickers, magnets, and bookmarks fit easily into an envelope.

❋ Email

Sometimes email is a preferred way to send longer messages and articles. You may need to text your older grandkids to let the know an email is coming!

❋ Audio Books

Numerous children's publications have a recording device that allows for you to read the book and send it to your grandkids. They will enjoy hearing your voice as they turn the pages.

❋ Technology Connections

Parents have busy schedules, so it may be helpful to set specific times for FaceTime or web chats. Or, if spontaneity works for both of your families, that is wonderful, too.

Grandparents Can Be Tech Savvy, Too!

There are many ways to stay in touch with your grandchild who may live far away. Keep in mind that the average attention span of a child is about one minute for each year of age. (a three-year-old's is about 3-4 minutes.) Experiment with different activities to meet the interests of your grandchild. As they get older, more variety will be possible. More ideas can be found in the Playbook.

❋ Sing a lullaby

❋ Play peek-a-boo

❋ Play music and sing songs together

❋ Make silly faces

❋ Read together

❋ Recite nursery rhymes

❋ Make and guess animal sounds

❋ Use puppets to chat

❋ Tell jokes or riddles

❋ Ask to see their schoolwork and offer homework help (except for math— unless you are a math teacher.)

❋ Share hobbies

❋ Play the guessing game

❋ Text, play online games, and share YouTube videos with older children. It can be engaging to connect with them on social media, if they are willing. Often games and/or events are live streamed.

The digital generation is quite tech savvy and Katie enjoys teaching her Nana Ruth Wiltz how to navigate the world of technology.

Being stuck in quarantine is frustrating, but my grandparents give me someone to talk to. Grandparents are great listeners. I am giving a shout out to my parents and grandparents who are there for me during this tough time.

Katie, at 14

There are educational word game apps that grandparents can play with their grands.

For example, Katie's tennis program has set up cameras at the courts and some practices can be viewed through YouTube.

Rachael, daughter

Extended Visits

Spending an overnight or several days at your home during parent vacations is a great time to enjoy activities mentioned in this book. Provide a journal so they can record their experiences. Many of the kid quotes in this book are from their journals and from extended visits. Be sure to search the house for that special duckie before they leave. A missing blankie can be traumatic—especially for the parents.

We took the twins on a day-trip to Peoria to visit my brother Steve, a Captain in the fire department.

If possible visit family members or friends at their workplace to provide invaluable experiences and treasured memories.

Grandma and Grandpa Camp

When my grandson was five years old, we began this tradition. We went out to lunch, to a children's museum, the community pool, and parks and playgrounds.

We also enjoyed Disney movies, sprinklers, and bubbles in the backyard, and exploring our yard.

—Jan Bowman, friend

Plan Trips Together

Take your grandchild on one of your vacations or plan a special trip just for them. There are many organizations that offer intergenerational programs. Road Scholar offers multigenerational family trips.

Our 8th grade graduation trips have been a treasured time with each grandchild. Ben was so excited about his trip to Washington, D.C. that he worked to persuade his cousin Samuel to choose that destination for his trip as well.

Ben chose our nation's capital for his 8th grade trip. Here he is with his grandpa at the Lincoln Memorial looking toward the Washington Monument.

16

Your Special Hot Sauce

Hot means full of spicy energy and enthusiasm. Make your sauce as hot as possible. The definition of play (frolic) is to "jump for joy" or to "move about energetically!" You are uniquely equipped to enrich your grandchild's life with your own hot version of energized play.

Integrating playfulness into your relationship with your grandchild is a purposeful, stimulating, and splendid responsibility. Play also brings great satisfaction. Don't be afraid of being silly or looking ridiculous. Have courage! This is the perfect opportunity for you to try new adventures. Romp like you have springs in your legs—even if they are bionic. Somehow grandkids bring out the desire to romp, even if it means you will challenge them to a race from your wheelchair. Of course, they will need to hop backwards or walk on their hands!

Feel the Humergy

The experience of vigorous, optimistic energy is called **humergy**. Facing tough stuff with a sense of humor is a powerful strategy for coping with life's challenges. Laughter reduces stress and depression. An ability to find the funny in life will help provide your very own spicy laughter legacy and serve as a model for your grandchild. Of course, often grandkids are the best source of humergy.

Some ideas to increase your humergy:

- Watch funny movies. Make a list of your favorites and share with your friends.

- Read humorous books or magazines. Include joke or riddle books.

- Share memes and funny posts on social media or in emails.

- Journal about the hilarious stuff. There is always a lot of that with grandkids.

- Find friends that make you laugh, and plan activities with them.

- Bring playfulness into your life (hula hoops and swings are a couple of my favorites!)

Remember what you did as a child that brought you joy and laughter. Try that activity again. My personal favorites were the swing and jumping on the pogo stick. I still absolutely love the energy I get from being on a swing and have five in our yard. The pogo stick is a great challenge and I laugh when I try to jump on it. My hula hoop skills are not what they used to be, however I can still make it go around for a bit. That playful activity brings me great delight.

> The grandparents have created many special memories for the kids by engaging in numerous fun experiences and activities. Whether it is a relaxing day at a park, a trip to the children's museum, exploring local festivals, or a day trip into Chicago, much fun is had by all!
>
> Jennifer, daughter-in-law

Emma loves hula hooping almost as much as I do! She challenged me to a hula hoop competition and easily completed more rotations than I did.

How Do You Find the Laughter in Your Life?

We learn from everything, even disasters in the kitchen.

Grandpa said I was old enough to have a tractor license. I got to ride on the tractor. Grandma pretended she was the police and asked to see my license. She is hilarious.

Faith, at 8

Celebrating Your Special Sauce Involves:

1. A willingness to try and learn about unusual things. My granddaughter Cloe was the reason that I learned about toad habitats, and together we built a toadarium.

2. A recognition that some plans might be too ambitious or may not work out. There are numerous times that my extraordinary planning vision did not match the reality of what really happened. A few words of wisdom:

   - Do not ever make cream puffs when you have several grandchildren who want to help.

   - Make sure you release captured insects from the Tupperware container before the next grandchild visit.

   - Limit the amount of softserve ice cream you give to a toddler.

   - Slime does not come out of hair very easily.

   - Green paint is the most difficult to remove from carpet—except for red or blue.

   - Mayonnaise takes crayon off of walls.

3. A purposeful determination to be playful.

   Look for ways to create surprises. My goal is to use my knowledge of play to plan experiential learning for the grandkids. I help my family when I include daily play in my own life.

   Don enjoys giving the grandkids rides on his small tractor and teaching them how to operate it. He asked 8-year-old Faith if she had a license to drive his tractor. She said no and looked a bit sad. I created a *Tractor Driver's License* that Don signed and she used it when riding with him.

4. Sharing your passions and interests with your grandkids.

   Playing outdoors, gardening, and art are hobbies of mine. Combining drama, nature, and art have contribute to my unique special sauce in creating relationships with my grandchildren.

5. Problem-based learning—this is simply a way to let the children decide on a project or activity they want to do and letting them figure out the details.

   The most ambitious activity was Bitty Baby and Bear's Wedding. This was a screenplay written by two sisters who decided that a doll and a stuffed animal wanted to get married.

playful

18

Laughter and Love

I am sure that as a parent, I did not spend enough time laughing and having fun with my own children. It is just an absolute joy to have time for laughing with our grandchildren. Making every effort to increase the laughter in your life will provide the ingredients for your own special hot sauce and for your unique recipe of delicious memories.

Your special sauce will be remembered for years to come!

We all have talents and gifts to share. Consider what you would enjoy sharing with your grandchild. I have had the unique opportunity of engaging with our amazing twelve grands to write this book. Their insights continue to inspire me, and I am grateful they have been willing to assist in this journey.

Experiential play is a critical component for learning. Play encourages the discovery skills that generate neural connections while promoting creativity, critical thinking, risk taking, and social bonding.

Free play is defined as child-directed rather than adult-directed. Choice, risk taking, and exploration are the foundation for humor development and form the basis for learning through play. This type of play is significantly important for adults as well. While many people assume that play is for children, our brains are really designed to play throughout our lives.

Left: The Circle Swing is a big hit with the grandkids (Emma and Christine on swing). Inset: Grandpa, with help from one of the grandkids, put up the swing so everyone can enjoy it.

My Special Sauce
ingredients:
play, laughter, and love.

Play everyday!

Play is not just for kids.
I am a REAL swinger!
We have 5 swings
in our yard.

19

Encourage Your Grandchild's Imagination

Bitty Baby and Bear's Wedding was a fairly elaborate activity that evolved over two days and included six cousins and several parents. It was created and planned with fairly elaborate details that included making food and decorations. Cousins were invited to help with preparations and parents were invited to the ceremony. The kids created invitations, went on a trip to the grocery store to purchase food, and cooked the reception treats. The final task before the ceremony included baking and decorating the wedding cake.

Guests were invited to the ceremony along with various stuffed animals and dolls who had speaking roles (enacted by cousins) and who played key roles in the ceremony. We dressed up in fancy clothing (old prom dresses, etc.) and tried on all of our costume jewelry to find the perfect combination. It was exciting and fun (and a bit exhausting) to coordinate this beautiful wedding.

Katie's Journal
Bitty Baby and
Bear's Wedding

Day 1: Preparations

Today I did a lot of wedding preparations. In fact, the whole day we worked on the wedding. We set up the altar downstairs and went to Schnucks to buy food. It was so much fun. We also made the two wedding (cake) toppers. We dipped gingerbread men in chocolate and are going to make them toppers. Tomorrow, Samuel and Christine are coming over to help. It is going to be the best wedding ever. We use fancy plates and picked out super fancy dresses. I picked out a silky black one and took diamond necklaces to go with it. We took practice runs 3 times. Luckily Platypus did not mess up his lines.

Day 2: The Big Day

Today was Bitty Baby's wedding. It was so much fun but very hard work. At 8:00 a.m. we went to pick up my cousins, Christine and Samuel. We got to work immediately. We made caramel apples. We dipped strawberries in chocolate and baked a cake. My list could go on forever. I was excited when the guests came. We went down to the altar and Platypus said a prayer and announced him and her, husband and wife. We came upstairs and ate our food and drank homemade punch. I loved the punch. After the wedding we went to the trampoline park. We bounced our hearts out and then went to dinner.

The wedding was wonderful, and the couple received a free 7-day vacation to Jamaica. Overall, it was a great time to spend with our cousins.

Samuel, at 12

Today we had a wedding. It was funny and serious.

Christine, at 11

You Are Invited

Service
Ceremony-Reader Platapus-Patty
Maid of Honor: Racooony
Best Man: Hippo
Bridesmaid: Whooper
Bridesmaid; Lucille
Bridesmaid: Cherry
Bridesmaid: Buckwheat
Groomsman: Snoot
Groomsman: Goaty
Groomsman: Ducky
Groomsman: Lammie
Flower Girl: Tracy

Reception Menu
Heart Shape Cheese and Crackers
Kebabs
Peanut Butter Sandwiches (Heart Shape)
Chocolate Covered Strawberries

love

On my 7th birthday this year at my party, I got many presents. Grandma gave me 7 presents for my 7th birthday. I really liked all of them. My favorite was "glow in the dark slime." I really liked unwrapping 7 presents and I had a great birthday party.

Faith, at 7

Practical Preparations: A Warm Welcome!

3

I t is a precious occasion when your grandchild visits your home for the first time. Savor this moment. Of course, it will be even more enjoyable if you are prepared. New parents are usually cautious and protective about the safety of their newborn. They will want to be assured that your home is safe, sanitary, and comfortable.

Consider these questions as you prepare your home for visits:

- How often will visits occur?
- What equipment might be needed?
- Is my home safe?

As a new parent, I remember cleaning my entire house with bleach to prepare for my own newborn's arrival. Covid-19 has made us more aware of the necessity for caution. Review and follow the recommendations of your local health agency. You will want to do a careful appraisal to get your home ready for safe, memorable visits.

I still had the crib that had been the sweet sleeping place for all four of my children. I was gently informed that the crib that had carefully held my babies was not recommended for my grandchildren. It seems that the slats need to be close enough that a soda can (2 3/8 inches apart) cannot get through. Since we started with grand twins closely followed by several additional grandbabies, we were fortunate to borrow a safety-approved crib and a Pack 'n Play®. That treasured crib was eventually used for the toddlers.

It was a surprise to learn that it was not just the crib, but there are many baby items that have expiration dates or are on recall lists. Check with the Consumer Product Safety Commission for details on recalls.

There are rainbows everywhere in this house.

Faith, at 4

While a blanket is essential, consider what additional investments you might want to make in preparation for visits. Of course, it depends on how often your grandchild will visit. Since we had little ones, there has been a major transformation in baby gear. I cringe when I remember how we transported our babies in the car. Car seats today are much safer, however, it can take an engineer to figure out how to install them.

There is a vast quantity of baby equipment on the market and it can be overwhelming to decide what would be useful. A practical option is to borrow larger items. Garage sales are a grandparent's dream. Amazing finds can include everything from gently used highchairs and bouncy seats to fantastic books and toys. Some babies will need adaptive equipment. Check with the parents for suggestions and recommendations.

While you may be eager for grandchild visits, you may live in an apartment or condo where a crying baby and noisy children are not exactly welcome. Plan a few adaptive strategies:

- Chat with the neighbors and introduce your adorable grandchild to them.
- Bring over cookies or banana bread.
- Wrap up a gift of ear plugs (kidding.)
- Invite your grandchild to create pictures for the neighbors.
- Take the baby for a stroller ride to nearby parks or nature areas.
- Arrange field trips to local museums, libraries, and sports centers.

From Formula to Finger Foods

The memories come back quickly! Your own parenting experience will help you determine if the cries mean hunger, an upset stomach, or exhaustion. Parents will bring frozen breast milk or formula with directions. Some have a philosophy of responsive feeding (attending to the baby's feeding cues). Other parents may prefer a set schedule and will write out detailed instructions. Keep a few extra bottles in reserve—not that any parent ever forgets to pack a bottle!

Isaiah enjoys the frosting on his birthday cake.

Different doctors seem to have diverse recommendations on when to start solid food. I remember my mom insisting that I start my babies on watery oatmeal at one month. While that concept seems inconceivable today, grandparents quickly realize that infant recommendations have evolved since their babies were born.

At some point it will be time for solid foods. You may want to invest in baby utensils and a dish. Some parents process their own fresh fruit and vegetables. Cheerios continue to be a favorite finger food. Do get some pictures of the spinach slithering out of their mouth.

Babies learn to prefer sweets at a young age. And grandparents have a fairly well-deserved reputation for giving kids cookies! It is pretty difficult to resist a huge grin and outstretched hand for a sugary treat. Many grandparents will keep cookies on hand, but it is important to initially offer other choices to entice healthier eating. Creating fruit "faces" or putting colorful sprinkles on oatmeal may tempt reluctant eaters. Read labels on products to be assured of nutritional value. Veggie chips are not as nutritious as they seem. Andrew does not like chocolate, so we usually make sure to serve both vanilla and chocolate flavors. However, the unanimous vote for the all-time favorite food at our house: home-made macaroni and cheese.

Steve wrote on his beautiful handmade Mother's Day card that he was thankful that grandma always made his favorite macaroni and cheese for family gatherings.

The Scoop on Poop

For newborns, the washer and drier topped with a foam pillow worked well as our changing table. A blanket on a bed or on the floor works, too. It was helpful to keep the following items on hand:

- Disposable diapers (pull ups for toddlers)

- Baby wipes

- Butt paste and butt paste spreaders (no kidding!)

- A few sleepers, onesies (and did I mention socks—lots and lots of socks?)

- A cloth diaper to throw over the little boy who chooses this diaper changing time to display his fountain creating skills.

Ah—that mysterious science of potty training. The process is easier if you have a small step stool, a potty seat, and books with wipeable covers. Techniques vary and of course the parents will have suggestions, or they may ask for advice. Some kids take to this with easy-peasy success and others are

Another huge blessing is that they were always prepared and ready for us to drop by. They kept extra clothes and diapers at their home. And by extra clothes I mean they had every size for every grandchild. It was wonderful! I never had to worry about forgetting things— cause with 4 kids, I'm always forgetting things!

Val, daughter-in-law

Aim for the Cheerios

Potty training hint for boys— put a cheerio in the toilet to encourage them to "try to hit the target."

My favorite memory is the duck song. We would all be in the tub and grandma would sing this song OVER AND OVER. Then we would get thrown to the lions. I just have so many memories.

Mimi at 7

Art by Katie, at 14

A stuffed lion our daughter Beth had given us became a favorite item. The younger kids would pounce on it after their bath as part of a bedtime routine. Recently, 8-year-old Isaiah discovered the lion again, brought it to the kitchen with him and announced that he had missed the lion and was glad to find it!

Don, author's husband

26

reluctant poopers. My granddaughter called me into the restroom telling me she needed a "wipe." I checked the toilet and exclaimed, "There is no poop in there." She replied, "But Grandma, I did a courtesy flush."

Some of the funniest moments with grandchildren have happened during toilet training. I had been casual, but firm in telling the boys to keep their penis down when sitting on the toilet. One of them passed by me in the bathroom and said, "Grandma, remember to keep your penis down!"

Bribery is wrong—except when it works to eliminate poopy diapers! When discussing potty training with my sister-in-law, Jeanette, I realized that her son was successfully using the potty before our son. Our boys were five days apart in age and as teachers, we had great fun sharing ideas, activities, and funny stories. Since my son had little interest in going to the potty, I asked her about their pooping success. As a side note, we had both been quite careful with limiting sweets in their diets. She reluctantly said that she was embarrassed to tell me that she had been giving an M&M as a reward. I laughed and needless to say—my son was soon receiving that small candy treat for pooping. Yep, a candy treat for a poop. What can I say?

A fingerplay or song during handwashing is a way to be sure they do a thorough job. My daughter Rachael taught her girls to sing the ABC song while washing their hands as it is the right length of time. Enticing soaps are a great incentive for handwashing. Cloe could not wait to wash her hands with the bar of clear soap that had a "fish" inside.

Isaiah was so happy to reunite with the lion!

Bath and Bubble Time

There is usually such delight in baby bath time. I found it handy to keep baby soap and shampoo available for those times they dumped the applesauce on top of their head or somehow got playdoh in their ear.

Bath time is a great place for teachable moments. Here, the twins learn how "to shave." Real shaving cream, toy shaver.

After enjoying a bath with bubbles and water toys, the grandkids would often be reluctant to get out of the tub. It became a tradition to wrap them in a towel and gently throw them on the bed with a large stuffed lion, teasingly saying, "I am going to throw you to the lion."

They always squealed and laughed when they knew they were going to be "tossed" into the lion's den. This made an easier transition from tub to bed and into pajamas.

Safety Checks: Home and Yard

I thought my house was clean until one of the babies picked up an overlooked paper clip on the floor and I noticed the dirty spots on the knees of that cute pink crawler! Safety concerns change through their ages and stages, but crawlers and toddlers require special precautions. They are quick! If you cannot constantly watch them every second, make sure they are in a gated or safe area.

Indoors

❋ Safety locks on cupboards are helpful as soon as crawling begins. Gate all stairways. Lock doors. Put bells on their shoes so you know where they are.

❋ Check the corners of desks and counters—if at eye height, you may want to cover them or put up a barrier.

❋ Keep bathroom doors shut. Some kids like to bathe in the toilet—especially on hot summer days.

❋ Put safety plugs in outlets. Secure the cords for blinds.

❋ Use extreme caution with space heaters, fans, and radiators.

❋ Scrapes are less painful when covered with a super-hero Band-Aid.

❋ Many plants (Easter Lilies and philodendrons, for example) can be poisonous if ingested. Check out the links of poisonous plants online. Keep the local safety hotline number handy, just in case your curious toddler eats something before you realize it.

❋ Peas in the nose or ears may require a trip to the ER.

❋ Cut grapes in half as whole grapes can be a choking hazard.

What happens if you touch electrictiy?

Sketch by Tyler (at 5) who quotes his father: "It is a juicy wire!"

GRANDMA HINT

Leave the locks off of one of the lower cupboards and fill it with plastic containers, cardboard boxes, and other odds and ends. They will love pulling everything out and playing with these on the floor. After emptying the containers, Andrew quickly crawled into the cupboard and proudly grinned at me.

Outdoors

❊ Enclosed decks are perfect for outdoor play. Put up gates or section off an area to keep kids contained. Some kids are actually Houdini-like escape artists. Chasing toddlers through the neighborhood might be a great workout, but a bit embarrassing in pajamas and slippers!

❊ Stollers and wagons can be a delightful way to travel around the yard and neighborhood. Be sure that the kids cannot climb or fall out. If going a distance, pack bottled water and wipes. Isaiah loved our trips to the neighborhood pond to feed oatmeal to the ducks.

❊ Plastic or blow up swimming pools are a must on hot days. Containers with over two inches of water should be emptied unless kids are being closely supervised. Fill the pool with funnels, balls, and plastic containers.

Grandma doesn't care if I go in the pool with all my clothes on!

Ready, Set, Transport

Often grandparents are asked to assume the role of "taxi driver" for their grandchild. Most parents will be especially grateful for assistance with trips to activities and to appointments.

Medical Permissions and Travel Permission

Our 13-year-old granddaughter Emma was with me when we were rear-ended. It was a fairly minor accident, but the police were called. I did not have her medical permission slip with me. The officer contended that he needed a permission slip, even though my granddaughter insisted she was fine. We were not allowed to leave the scene until he called an ambulance for paramedics to check on her. When the medics arrived (2 hours later), they took her blood pressure—that was it! An unexpected bonus was the ETs were young and personable, and increased her interest in the medical field. When traveling long distances, it is a good idea to have a travel permission form with you.

Determination, energy, and courage appear spontaneously when we care deeply about something. We take risks that are unimaginable in any other context.

—Margaret Wheatley

GRANDMA HINTS

When emptying the pool, I was chagrined to see that mold had grown on the inside of some of the containers. Those items made a quick trip to the dishwasher.

• • • • • • • • • • • • • • • •

Keep medical and travel permission slips in the car, purse, and/or diaper bag. These forms may need to be notarized depending on where you live.

Car Seats

While booster seats are easy to move from car to car, transferring the infant seat can be difficult and time consuming. Since we often ended up as "designated" drivers, we were grateful to have our own infant seat that we could keep in the car. This was one of the best presents I ever received for Mother's Day from my son, Andy. Be sure to check out car seat laws in your state, as there are often weight and age regulations.

Supplies for the Distance Warrior

My daughter-in-law, Jennifer gave me a tote bag with her children's handprints painted on it. What a wonderful and thoughtful gift that turned out to be! I keep it in the car to hold essential age-appropriate items needed for travel near and far.

Items to include:

- Tissues
- Band-Aids
- Baby wipes
- Gum for older kids
- Diapers
- Bucket—some of my grandchildren get car sick…sigh
- Wipes—never too many!
- Snacks (parent approved)
- Baby bottle, water bottle or drink boxes
- Books and toys
- Change of clothes
- Medical Consent Forms
- Plastic bags—did I mention that some of my grandchildren get car sick?

Find the Laughter!

If your baby is "beautiful and perfect, never cries or fusses, sleeps on schedule and burps on demand, an angel all the time," you're the Grandma.

Theresa Bloomingdale

At our garage sale, we tried to sell the caterpillar toy because it made annoying noises whenever it detected motion. It made us laugh!

A Parent Haven

Grandparents have a wonderful opportunity to help parents with the little ones. Find ways to create a mini retreat for the parents when they come to your home; give them a few minutes to read or take a walk. It doesn't take long for these parents to close their eyes in the recliner while I take the kids on a nature walk.

It's a win-win for everyone—parents get a break from their everyday busy-ness, and grandparents get to enjoy all the childhood fun we sometimes forget we love so much!

As a full-time working mom with four kids, I'm always running somewhere! When I come to their home, I love that I get to sit in a recliner, read a newspaper, and drink iced tea. They give me a little break from the chaos of the everyday. It really is the best!

Val, daughter-in-law

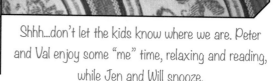

Shhh...don't let the kids know where we are. Peter and Val enjoy some "me" time, relaxing and reading, while Jen and Will snooze.

Happy Trails!

Exploring nature is a great way to spend time with the grandkids.

While parents are relaxing in the house, the children spend time with us outside in the garden, at the park, or on a hike. There is never a shortage of things to do outside!

Clockwise from left: Exploring Anderson Japanese Gardens in Rockford; Hiking at Rock Cut State Park; Stopping to pick the flowers; Night walks are an adventure!

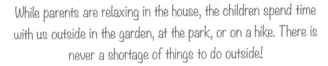

It is fun to fly kites
with my cousins.
Kites go way up in the air,
especially if it is windy
and you jog.

Isaiah, at 9
Artwork by Christine, at 13

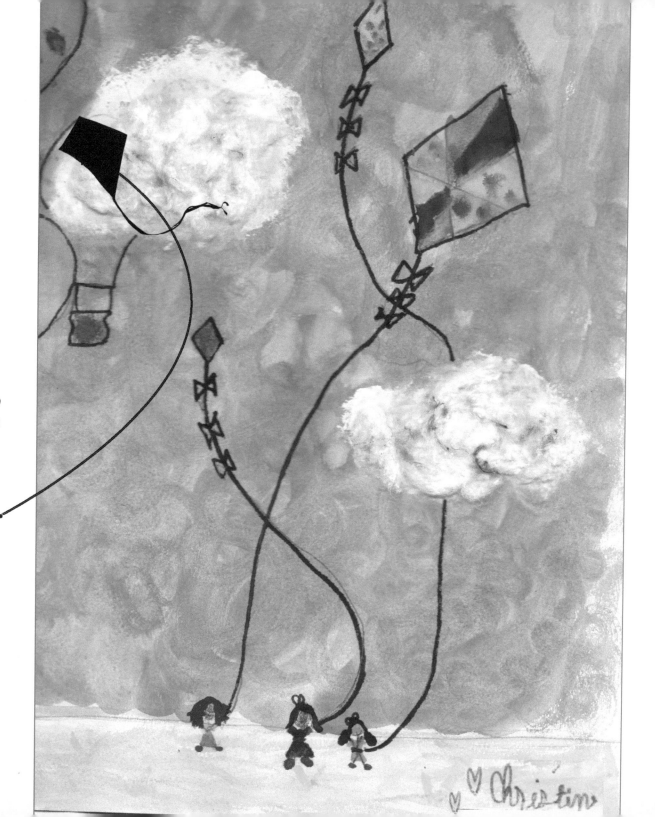

Nourishing the Apple on the Family Tree

4

A grandchild is a living reflection of previous generations. Your heritage is a unique and priceless gift. During your grandparenting journey, there may be unexpected moments when you feel touched by the blessings and spirit of past generations. You might actually feel the presence of your father as you cradle this little one. Those treasured metaphysical moments will stimulate a deep desire to share your family history with your grandchild.

At some point your grandchild will be curious about their family tree. There are two significant things to remember as you share your genealogy. As with the twin "Things" in Dr. Seuss Cat in the Hat book these are two reminders that both emotions and interactions can provide mischief and unexpected fun. These will serve as a core guide in creating your own extraordinary legacy of laughter.

> THING 1: **Emotions play a critical role in memory.**
>
> Memories of your heritage have been forged over the years by emotional connections with your family. Reflect on what you know of your family history and determine how you can best merge old memories into new experiences for your grandchild.
>
> THING 2: **Positive interactions will create a lifetime of memories.**
>
> Purposeful planning will ensure the transition of your living memories to your grandchild. As you and your grandchild create your own cherished stories, record them so that those treasured laughter-filled memories will be saved for future generations.

The history of grandparents is remembered in the laughter of their children and their children's children.

Charles and Ann Morse

If you look deeply into the palm of your hand, you will see your parents and all generations of your ancestors.

Thich Nhat Hanh

Roots and...

My dad and me!

The author

Your home will hold many memories for your grandchild from your visits. Sights, sounds and smells will be triggers for memories of time with you. "This smells like Grandma's House!" exclaimed eight-year-old Faith in a contented tone when coming to our house after a long Covid separation.

Flashback to the time spent with your own grandparents. What thoughts immediately come to mind? Focus on your feelings. Since our most vivid memories are usually linked to strong emotions, what you remember may surprise you. Recollections can be triggered in a variety of ways including sensory experiences that involve music, aroma, or actual physical sensations. It is intriguing to recognize that the memories we retain may be based on both positive and negative/traumatic experiences. It is often a mystery as to why a specific memory is permanently stored in our brain, but chances are it is associated with a powerful feeling.

I have vague memories of interactions with my grandparents. My recollections are a disjointed assortment of sensations that include sights and smells.

I recall making cookies with my dad's mother. I can actually visualize the flour and rolling pin along with a distinct awareness of being in that kitchen. These are pleasant memories and that cookie recipe is still a treasured part of my recipe collection. The most enduring image that I have of my grandmother is one of her lying on a couch during our visits. The memory is one of her sad demeanor and this image continues to haunt me. She was doted on by my grandfather, a thin, bald, serene man. When he babysat for us, we were entertained with the cigarette smoke rings he produced while exhaling smoke. He played a small harmonica to entertain us.

> I have vague memories of my grandparents. My recollections are a disjointed assortment of sensations that include sights and smells.

Our family picnics were held at their home and jam-packed with delicious food always followed by grandpa slicing a juicy watermelon. Spitting seeds in the grass made him smile in delight. With 30 grandchildren, there were usually spirited softball games with my cousins, but not much one-on-one time with my grandparents. There are a few funny and embarrassing stories that have been conveyed from my parents. The most captivating one for

34

Branches

My mom and me!

me, occurred at their wedding. Apparently, my grandmother walked down the aisle wearing a coat hanger that was still in the back of her dress. No wonder she did not like having her picture taken. I do treasure a photo of her at the baptism of my oldest son. She made the trip with my parents to see her great grandchild. I was so glad she did, as it was the last time that I saw her.

My mother's parents lived in Germantown, Illinois, which was a three-hour seemingly endless journey for us from Peoria. Grandma Duncan was always delighted to see us, welcoming us with a hug after wiping flour-covered hands on her apron. The aroma of freshly baked pies on the sun porch always greeted us. Shortly after we arrived, we would run out to the yard that had a grape arbor, a well with a pump, a hammock, and an intriguing outhouse (no longer functional except as a "playhouse" for my sister and me.) My grandmother laughed when she realized that we were playing in that rickety, wooden building with the half-moon on the door.

I do not remember having any actual playtime with these grandparents either. Peeling bushels of peaches on the back porch was indicative of the strong work ethic that was woven into our visits. There were a few times that my sister Nancy and I were invited by Grandma to eat in the dining room with the adults instead of at the kid's table in the kitchen. This milestone event was accompanied by a feeling of pride in being considered a grown-up.

After supper, Grandpa would sit in the recliner and watch *The Lawrence Welk Show* while the women did the dishes. There was usually a lot of laughing while completing this "woman's work" with my aunts.

My most vivid memory of our visits was when Grandma got upset with Grandpa for farting loudly at the table. He unabashedly said it was a natural thing and dismissed her disdainful comment with a wave of his hand. I was careful not to laugh out loud, but I remember being astonished by that exchange.

Grandpa was proud of his stamp collection. He gave me some first issue stamps, which I keep as a treasured memory of my time with him.

> Grandma Duncan was always delighted to see us, welcoming us with a hug after wiping flour-covered hands on her apron.

The Mix: Genealogy and Experiences

Both nature (genealogy) and nurture (environment) affect the development of a sense of humor. Your sense of humor has been forged by this combination. What is your temperament? Were your parents serious or playful? Did they engage your sense of humor and encourage play experiences or was your childhood more serious or even traumatic? The ability to laugh through adversity nurtures resilience. You may have found that your sense of humor helped you survive some rough times.

Your sense of humor is a kaleidoscopic mix of innate personality with the environmental influence of one's village. A mindful awareness of your own sense of humor will have a powerful impact on how you connect with your grandchild and on your legacy for them.

We know from brain science that the most powerful way children learn is experientially through play. Humor, laughter, play, and joy can be intentionally incorporated as an essential part of nurturing your grandchild. The positive emotional impact from playful interactions will leave a heartprint, a legacy of memories that will last a lifetime.

Nature: Humor and Heredity

Are we born with a sense of humor? A glimpse into the research on temperament provides convincing evidence that many of the characteristics of our *humor being* emerge from our biological disposition. Those innate individual differences usually remain somewhat constant throughout our life.

If you are the parent of more than one child, you will have noticed individual differences among siblings from birth. Comments are often made at family gatherings about how a child resembles another family member—either in physical features or in temperament. Inherited family traits are sometimes quite obvious.

It made me chuckle when my son mentioned how his energetic boy reminded him of his own childhood. This toddler had just managed to scatter toys and food all over the kitchen floor with one quick swoop. We laughed together as we thought of his own amusing childhood escapades. It reminded us of the frequent quote, "The apple does not fall far from the tree." I know our grandson will grow into an amazing man, just like his father.

An exploration of genealogy and your DNA can contribute to a deeper understanding of inherited characteristics and of your ancestry. We are beginning to understand the profound impact our own grandparents had on our physiology. Exploring family history together can enrich the interactions with your grandchild while inspiring personal reflections.

Nurture: Treasured Traditions

Humorous stories and generational folk tales are an engaging way to bring your ancestors to life. It is a grandparent privilege to trace and share family heritage. Looking through old picture albums is an invaluable reminder of your history. Unfortunately, I was not too interested in my own family history until after my grandparents had passed away. My mother did a notable job of keeping pictures and describing family stories, but I wish I had asked them more questions and recorded their memories.

Preserve Your History in Photo Scrapbooks

In today's electronic age, it's more common to keep photos digitally on a computer or smartphone. But, there is nothing like sitting on a couch with your grandchildren and showing them their history in a scrapbook.

Mom and her siblings

Family lore has it that Richard Duncan is second from the right in the front row at this saloon

My grandma Veronica Duncan with my mom (Ruth Wiltz) on the left; Uncle Jerome on the right

From an early age, kids can learn about the importance of the family history; Great, great grandma Veronica Duncan was the first woman in Germantown, Illinois to drive a model T like this one.

37

The treasured Duncan nativity built by my great great grandfather sits on our piano over the holidays.

Stories Through the Generations

Ancestry: The Story of Your Grandparents and Previous Generations

❋ Research and record your family history.

Identify resources available for tracing and preserving your heritage. Make sure family photos are organized and digitized for each child and grandchild.

❋ Create a photo book, power point or flash drive for each child with diagrams of the family tree.

Include the stories of great Uncle Gene, Aunt Anne and all of the noble, notable, and notorious relatives. The story of one of our infamous relatives was found in an intriguing 1874 newspaper clip "Killed in a Blow; The Terrible and Sudden Death of Richard Duncan." The article details a well-respected saloon-keeper, Richard Duncan (my great, great grandfather) who was drawn into a fight with a customer. Apparently, this man ran away after he had thrown Richard to the "ground striking his head violently against the curb.", Unfortunately Richard died the next day.

❋ Identify heirlooms and other mementos:

When I was a child, we celebrated Christmas by putting up the stable made of sticks that was built circa 1880 by mom's grandfather, T.J. Welling. The nativity figures are old, chipped, and mismatched. I am sure my six siblings and I added a few chips over the years, and I am even more certain my four children did. However, each chip is a reminder of how this nativity has been treasured and set up every Christmas, its history shared through the generations. The stable has traditionally been passed onto the oldest daughter in the Duncan family.

❋ Plan for the distribution of collections and mementos:

As I was dusting the beautiful cup and saucer collection from my grandmother, I realized that I wanted each of my granddaughters to have one. Together we planned a tea party. We made the treats including chocolate covered strawberries and blueberry scones. The table was set with their very own cup and saucer. We sipped hot tea and enjoyed the goodies served on fancy plates. Faith was a baby so her older sister chose a tea set for her. After the party, I put their birth order number on the bottom of their chosen cups with a plan to give them at a future special occasion.

❋ Tag treasures

If one of the grandchildren privately admires something, you might put their name or "birth order number" on the bottom of that piece. If you have more than one grandchild, make sure

Let's  Party

My grandmother's heirloom tea cups will eventually be given to my granddaughters. The tea party was a special way to celebrate and honor the gifts passed down from one generation to the next.

Picking wildflowers for the table.

Welcome to the Family, FAITH!

Serving homemade treats . . .

enjoying time with cousins . . .

and setting a beautiful table.

A Veteran's Story
By Cloe, at 11

William James Wiltz is my great-grandfather. He is not here anymore, but my grandma knows a lot about her father's time in the military. That is why I interviewed her. My great-grandfather was in World War II. He was in the Army. He served from 1942 to 1945.

My great-grandfather was a sergeant and he handed out uniforms. When my great-grandfather was at war, he saw many dead people. He did not like seeing that. He also got malaria right before the Normandy Invasion. The man who went in for him during the Invasion was killed. If my great-grandfather would not have gotten malaria, I probably would not be here today.

that each child has a couple of things that are designated for them. I also put a number on the bottom of beautiful items that were given to me by my own children, so those will go back to their kids someday.

Your Story: Memories from Your Youth

✳ Preserve collections
My father served in WWII. His gray, battered army trunk was filled with mementos from the war including the bronze star. My mother kept his medals along with news clippings and three years of precious love letters. My 11-year-old grandson, Steve, was especially interested reading the newspapers and in hearing his war stories but was not too interested in the love letters.

✳ Recall family fables
Elaborate on some of those weird stories that seem to take on increasingly exaggerated proportions. Embellishing family stories so they become legendary is a memorable way to bring family characters to life.

I remember my Uncle John recalling how they had to walk barefoot to school 10 miles in the snow—uphill both ways. When my brother, Richard, visited their hometown and saw their home and the school, he asked, "So, where is that hill?" Uncle John also had a complete set of stories that all started with, "We were so poor that…"

✳ Video tape the relatives telling stories
It is captivating to watch your grandchild interview an aunt or great uncle. They can often extract details that you have not heard before.

✳ Teach family games and activities from your childhood
Do your grandchildren know how to skip to double-dutch or play kick the can?

✳ Play games!
Games were a huge part of my life as a child. My father passed along his love of pinochle to many of us. The comical comments that he made during card games have also been passed along. And since he taught my children how to play, and we currently have several generations playing this game together, our grandchildren are now repeating some of his humorous gestures and sayings.

❋ Share stories, toys, pictures, and mementoes from your childhood
We chuckled as we watched the grandkids trying to figure out how to operate the old rotary phone found in a box in the basement.

Your Children's Mementoes (Your grandchild's parents)

❋ Dig out pictures of your kids when they were little
Label these precious keepsakes (hopefully, you can recall when and where they were taken.)
These old pictures can be scanned, digitally saved, and even published in a memory book.

❋ Sort through that shoebox filled with childhood videos
Label and digitize. Create a master video, pop some popcorn and show it at a family movie night. Give a digital copy to each grandchild as a keepsake.

Art by Christine

Cards and board games provide hours of family fun!

The Great Math Chicken Challenge!

One Christmas, my brother Richard gave me a large light-up rooster. Since I enthusiastically admired it, I have been receiving interesting and fun chickens from him every year. I now have a collection of more than 50 chickens in my kitchen.

I challenged the grandchildren to figure out how many roosters each will get if we ever move. I call it **The Great Math Chicken Challenge!** Count the roosters and divide by 12 grandchildren.

I hope some of the grandkids will want the 27 cute frogs, too.

By Stephen

Capturing Memories for Future Generations

My only birthday request every year is that we get together for family pictures. This is one of my favorites photos from *Picture Day*. These photos reveal Don's valiant efforts of experimenting with a wide variety of photo backdrops and activities. Some ideas have worked better than others. The ambitious pyramid pose was a disaster. We never did get a good picture as the structure kept collapsing amid giggles and groans.

We usually use our annual pictures for our holiday greeting card. We have tried various techniques of grouping families, so it is easier to determine which child belongs to which family.

❋ Hula away with a Hawaiian party theme with leis, colorful dresses, shorts, and fun shirts.

❋ Throw some shade with sunglasses and derby hats.

❋ Dress in matching T-shirts or pajamas.

❋ Balloons! Make sure you have plenty, as my kids (not the grandkids, mind you) had fun blowing them until they burst. Of course, some of the best pictures were of the popping effects.

❋ Stage some pictures of the grandkids holding a star or another item with their birth order number. Thanks to our daughter-in-law, Jennifer, who shared this creative numbering idea.

❋ Set up a photo booth. Set out a variety of hats, beads, leis, bandanas, sunglasses and dress up clothes. Encourage creating crazy, funny poses.

❋ Plan for each child to be photographed with significant relatives.

❋ Take pictures of each individual child doing a favorite activity.

❋ Invite the kids to "ham it up" with goofy expressions and poses before the actual picture to have a better chance of getting a smile.

I have taken family pictures for the last 20 years. Mary Kay gets costumes and poses the family members for the shots. The whole operation reminds me of trying to herd cats. Some of the biggest offenders for crazy antics are the fathers!

Don, husband

Picture Day!

Wrangling four families and 12 grandchildren to take a family photo is no small feat. But, every year, we manage to get it done, leaving a legacy of laughter and treasured memories.

Samuel enjoys fingerpainting with shaving cream.

Rituals and Traditions

Greetings

Establishing small rituals can create ginormous bonds that include joy and laughter. Whenever I see Cloe she says, "Grandma. Grandma. Grandma." And I respond with, "Cloe. Cloe. Cloe!" I am not sure how this ritual started, but we both laugh every time we share this greeting with each other. She even signs her name, "Cloe. Cloe, Cloe."

When Katie and I are together, we sing "Joy to the fishes in the deep blue sea, joy to you and me." At first it was just a fun song we used as a greeting. Now it is a well-established ritual that lightens my mood every time we see each other.

Faith (7 years) and I went on errands together. We found a cute goose dressed in yellow with an umbrella. I bought it for her to remind her that she is "sunny and funny." When I see her, I say "sunny" and she laughingly responds with "funny!"

Grandma Days

Family events are magnificent opportunities for creating memories. However, if you have several grandchildren, it is great to get to know each grandchild with a special time just for them. Whenever possible, plan a distinctive day for each child. Our family calls these *Grandma Days*.

Favorite things
to do on
Grandma Days

- Baking cookies
- Making crafts
- Pictures
- Games

Steve, at 9

Kids can help plan these special days, but they also delight in knowing there are secret activities, too. They love to guess what surprises will be part of their special day. A *Grandma Day* is a great opportunity for individual activities that might not be easy with several grandchildren.

Faith enjoys stirring the batter on Grandma Day.

Grieving

Rituals can provide an opportunity to teach grandkids about using humor to cope with loss. Grieving can be experienced during the loss of a boyfriend or in the heartbreaking death of a family member.

Laughter often emerges during memorial services when stories are told. And have you observed how frequently a sense of humor is mentioned in obituaries?

When we pass by a cemetery, we have taught the grandkids to repeat my father's jokes about graveyards. "That's the last place I want to go. I hear people are dying to get in there." At first, the grandkids were somewhat shocked… but it is an invaluable opportunity to let them know that laughter can be found everywhere.

My father really enjoyed sharing that play on words and repeated it EVERY single time we passed a cemetery. When he died, his children and grandchildren created a poster board with all of his unique and crazy quotes alongside his pictures. It was a great opportunity to share laughter while grieving his loss, and it helped his grandchildren realize that humor can be an effective coping strategy.

Encourage children to express their feelings through art.
Emma, at 14, painted this piece during the pandemic quarantine.

During the Covid-19 pandemic, our families felt a deep sadness when we could not get together. Most were also experiencing the loss of school and not being able to participate in sports. While it can be difficult to provide support from a distance, technology is helpful for sharing pictures and feelings during challenging times. We talked, texted, and cried about missing each other, our losses, and our grief.

Grandparents can be quiet listeners, recognizing the sense of loss by listening to and acknowledging feelings of anger and sadness. Care packages can be sent to let the kids know you are thinking of them.

The Healing Power of Humor

Whenever I need support in the grieving process, I reread the book Navigating Grief with Humor by my dear friend Dr. Melissa Mork.
I highly recommend this book for additional ways to process the pain and support family members.

Grandma helped us create a funeral for a dead bird. In this situation we learned about loss. When I found the bird, I was very upset. This was one of my very first experiences with the death of an animal. This burial gave me a sense of closure.

Katie, at 14

45

Join in the Fun!

Reunions: Celebrating Generational Bonds

❋ Involve your grandchild in planning family get togethers

❋ Plan a scavenger hunt. The *Spy Scavenger Hunt* was a huge success.

- Form teams—include adults
- Hide things in the yard—use cell phones to take action pictures

❋ Create centerpieces with old family photos.

❋ Produce a power point or movie to share.

❋ Invite various family groups to do a group improv, song, or tribute. Our family did a quick and easy routine for my Aunt Rosemary Duncan when she turned 90 years old. It was a simple tipping of derby hats towards my aunt with a "Happy Birthday" message.

Family Fun!

More than 100 people gathered for the Duncan Family Reunion honoring our aunt, Sister Rosemary, for her 90th birthday party!

Preserving Your Legacy

Take photos to create an annual memory book for your grandchild of your experiences together. Keep your cell phone handy to capture the unexpected and funny selfies together.

Your experiences of joy, laughter, and play will leave a lasting legacy in a child's memory bank. They will think you are the most special grandma in the world when you share laughter and love with them.

Left: I love to play with my grandchildren: in a boat, in a car, on a trampoline—we have fun wherever we are!

Top: Isaiah sharing his memory book with his family; bottom: Tyler and Ben with their memory books.

One tradition Don and Mary Kay started was creating a special photo album for each grandchild and presenting it to them each year at Christmas. These albums, beautifully and thoughtfully created, highlight pictures from special events throughout the year. I am so thankful for these albums, and I love pulling them off the shelf to reminisce, laugh, and reflect (and maybe shed a tear or two) over how fast the kids have grown!

Jennifer, daughter-in-law

Grandma is full of funny.
She is not like other grandmas.
She goes to fun places with us.
She climbs on rock walls,
jumps on trampolines.
She is the best grandma.

Cloe, at 8

47

TREE CLIMBING
MADE POSSIBLE
BY ANDREW

Grandpa built a ladder with some of the kids to make it easier to get into our willow tree. I cleared the branches out of the willow tree and created a sign for climbing.

Andrew, at 13

Presence Over Presents

5

Your children and grandchildren are an integral part of your very being, and their impact on the world is intimately connected to you. Your purposeful presence will endure as a treasured memory and last far longer than any purchased present (unless, of course if you give them a real car—they will remember a real car). Playful moments trigger laughter and that laughter will be a highlight of your time together. Capture it by taking a picture of the moment. Even babies will appreciate seeing pictures of the two of you laughing together. Reliving those lighthearted moments will generate positive feelings of joy over and over again.

The Ultimate Present is Your Presence

From the moment this infant is born, your loving energy is a vital part of their life. You will make a difference in both the everyday and the extraordinary moments you share with your grandchild.

Participate in as many activities as possible from play dates to pre-school concerts. As they grow older and become more involved in extracurricular activities, request their schedules. There is nothing quite like actually being there to applaud their efforts and delight in their accomplishments.

Arrive early to their events to get good seats. Where in the world did all of these other grandparents come from? Of course, you will take lots of pictures. Do not post on social media unless you have parent and grandchild permission. Enthusiastically join in the cheering! (Unless at a golf tournament—I found out from Andrew that I could get kicked off the course for cheering).

If you cannot attend an event, ask parents to send pictures and/or video so you can engage in a follow-up conversation. Technology makes it possible to live stream events, so you can be virtually present for their performance.

Share your presence in every way that you can. You will make a difference in both the everyday and the extraordinary moments with your grandchild.

49

Grandmas

Dedicated to Mary Kay Morrison

Grandmas do many things.
Clean your boo boos,
Pull your strings.
They will love you
even if you're bad.
They cheer you up
when you are sad.
They teach you what is
right and just.
They make sure you're clean,
with not a speck of dust.
My grandma makes me happy.
We watch the birds and dew.
That's because
grandmas need loving, too.
And no other grandma is as
sweet as you.

Written by Katie, at 8

Grandparents Have Bragging Rights

What a blessing that we view our grandchildren through rose-colored glasses. It is a powerful opportunity and sacred responsibility to support their talents and abilities. In addition to attending their events, let them know that you believe in their abilities. Display what they make or give to you. BRAG about their achievements. It is a grandparent's duty to do so!

* Clip their "Picasso" onto a clothesline hung around the kitchen or family room wall (thanks to daughter-in-law, Val for this ingenious idea).

* Frame their artwork and display it. We created a Grandchild Hall of Frames in the playroom. Garage sales are a thrifty place to find those frames for their creations.

* Keep stickers and small gifts to send via snail mail when they achieve something special or to accompany a get-well message.

* Call or text to congratulate them on a successful sporting event, for passing a difficult test or for being chosen to do a solo.

* Hang pictures, artwork, and other stuff on your refrigerator. Buy another refrigerator if you do not have enough space.

After a family party, there was a tiny post-it-note on the counter with the lemon bars from 9-year-old Cloe who wanted to be sure I had gotten some of the desert their family had made: "4 lemon bars left–I love you" That little memo has been posted on my fridge for several years and always makes me smile. Cloe laughed when she saw it still posted a year later. She could not believe that I had kept that sweet reminder of her kindness.

50

Be the Present

Many toy rooms are filled with unused playthings. Some of the best gift ideas include being the present! Spending time together is the ultimate gift. You can ask the parents for ideas and/or you can give your grandchild choices of what they would like to do to celebrate.

Birthday Presence

Birthdays come quickly. With each one, you will be wondering how the time passed so quickly. That toy may be enjoyed for a few months, but your presence is the present that will be long remembered.

Samuel has long been interested in knowing that my father served in World War II. We had often looked at some of the pictures. For his 13th birthday, we went to the Chicago Museum of Science and Industry and toured the WWII submarine and other exhibits. We found a book with details about the role of submarines during the war. Since my husband, Don was a middle school history teacher, his expertise was invaluable in the discussions. Lifelong memories were created with the museum visit and by sharing some of our family's military history.

General ideas for creating gift-giving memories include:

* Art, music, sports classes

* Gift cards to bookstores; magazine subscription

* Tickets for a trip with you to a play, or museum, or sky-diving (kidding)

* Game or Movie Night: Give a ticket with a specific date for a game night with you.

Take the Kids Shopping

Shopping with a tweenager at a unique store is always a fun option. Steve introduced me to Hobby Town, which had a lot of really fun playful toys for both of us. We also enjoyed a trip to Dick's Sporting Goods to search for fishing lures. Some of the teens enjoy a shopping trip to try on and model clothes.

Of course, we do give traditional gifts. Consumable items are often most welcome by the parents. These include crazy socks, gloves, and of course-gift cards. I have found it helpful to store small fun gift items, so I am ready for upcoming birthdays. Gifts of slime, playdoh, and art supplies offer opportunities for stress relief. Books, flashlights, kites, and binoculars are great options to include for special occasions.

> It was so much fun to have time with Grandma for my birthday. It was fun to get some new clothes, and we had some ice cream after shopping. We got these bubble gum squishy balls, and they were so funny.
>
> Mimi, at 14

> On my 7th birthday this year at my party, I got many presents. Grandma gave me 7 presents for my 7th birthday. I really liked all of them. My favorite was "glow in the dark slime." I really liked unwrapping 7 presents and I had a great birthday party.
>
> Faith, at 7

Community Presence

The Neighborhood

Chances are your grandchildren will be riding bikes and skateboarding in your neighborhood. Introduce them to the neighborhood kids and, if feasible, invite those children over to play.

Your Town/City/State

Sometimes we forget about the fantastic opportunities in our own communities. Connect with the Chamber of Commerce and local tourism centers for information about resources and events. Look into grandparent passes at local venues.

A fun time at the Boone County Fair.

* Visit local parks, nature centers, and forest preserves.

* Explore museums.

* Try your skill at a miniature golf course.

* Attend county fairs. There are usually special days for kids.

* Bounce at the trampoline park.

* Fall into fun at an ice-skating rink. Many rinks now have "walkers" to avoid falling!

* Experience rock climbing at an indoor facility or at a state or national park.

* Jump into sky diving (OK—this requires more courage than this author has).

The Nicholas Conservatory in Rockford, Illinois is a favorite place for the grandkids.

Country and World

Take day trips with your grands to learn about and explore historic destinations. Traveling with your grandchild offers new learning experiences for both of you. There are numerous intergenerational programs available. Don's experience as a history teacher proved invaluable in planning our trips.

✳ Share your personal travel experiences.

✳ As you travel, take pictures of funny signs and unusual art that reflect cultural and ethnic differences and text to your grandkids. Humor transcends boundaries and laughter language is universal.

✳ Send postcards: Print address labels before the trip and purchase postcard stamps to bring along. Most hotel clerks will be happy to mail these.

✳ Bring home small souvenirs (with 12 grands, we had to be creative in finding mementos.)

  • Find keepsakes that represent that area. In Norway, we found tiny trolls thanks to planning assistance from our friend Harald Ellingsen.

  • Collect rocks for each child. (make sure collecting is permitted). Put them in a rock garden or use them for a craft project. If collecting shells, make sure to wash them thoroughly before packing them. (of course, I realized this invaluable advice when I was overcome by the stench from the shells in my suitcase upon arriving home.)

  • Find food items that are unique for that country (for example, Swiss chocolate, Swedish fish candy).

  • Notice and gather items unique to that country. It is fun to observe and share interesting disposables like napkins or hotel soaps that are written in a different language. Kids will enjoy seeing coins from other countries and they will be curious about their value.

> Don's (grandpa) knowledge of history keeps the kids engaged now that they are older.
>
> Julie, daughter-in-law

> Recently, I went with Grandma to the Chicago Art Institute. We studied different artists and works of art. It was fun.
>
> Samuel, at 13

The Giving Presence: Sharing Beliefs and Values

Sharing time and resources with the less fortunate in your family and community is an invaluable opportunity for conversations about values and social justice.

❋ Visit shut-ins (check with the agency for guidelines and to set a time for a visit).

❋ Provide the materials for grands to create bookmarks to share with residents and their caregivers.

❋ Bake bread together, wrap with ribbon and bring with you when you visit.

❋ Pack a book for the grandchild to read out loud to the resident.

❋ Invite the recipient of your visit to share their life stories.

❋ Choose a puzzle or game that can be enjoyed together and left at the facility.

❋ Participate in a food drive.

❋ Volunteer for the homeless or pet shelter.

❋ Support school fundraisers.

❋ Volunteer in a neighborhood school (read, tutor, donate).

Share the Laughter

Recently, my brother and I helped Grandma in one of her humor workshops at a local nursing home. Our job was to help set up, welcome and talk to people, and help her whenever she needed it.

Everyone there was enthusiastic and it was obvious that the residents enjoyed themselves and had a wonderful time!

I was glad to have this opportunity to bring a little bit of laughter to this nursing home and I'd do it again anytime!

Christine, at 13

Left: Helping at the Humor Workshop. Above: Faith and Isaiah bring flowers to the residents of a local nursing home. Illustration at right was created for a Grandparent Open House at school.

Christine, at 8

The Full Circle of Presence

Grandchildren love to be your helper. From the time they are small, they will love assisting you with household chores. It gives them a sense of being needed and provides the joy that comes from productive work.

As you age, your grandchildren may become an increasingly important supportive presence in your life. If your health prohibits you from doing certain chores or activities, invite your grandchild to help with your needs. They will usually be eager to help. A sense of caring and responsibility is generated whenever you ask for their assistance. This full circle of a loving relationship is especially poignant with a grandchild.

Help in the Yard and Garden

Steve roto-tilled my new garden plot and Mimi helped to plant it. Andrew, Christine and Samuel helped to haul and rake lime for the paths. Christine helped me stain our new "troll bridge."

Samuel and Christine help load brush.

Can you find the troll?

Christine's handiwork on the troll bridge.

In asking for their help, you are validating a mutually beneficial relationship of love and respect.

Helping the grandkids work on a project has been a great way to get closer to them as well as teach them new skills. Ironically, I now call on them to do things that I can't do myself.

Don, husband

56

Help with Household Chores

We were feeling a bit overwhelmed in getting ready for the annual Easter celebration. Our 17-year-old twins, Ben and Tyler offered to help fill Easter eggs. Afterwards, Ben helped build a potting bench. Tyler sanded some old green metal tables and painted them. They not only helped lift stones in the garden, they lifted our spirits as well.

Assistance with a Garage Sale

We knew we needed to get rid of some of the stuff that just seems to randomly multiply. Garage sales can be an awesome family event. They convey the value of recycling, teach business skills and increase the opportunity for meeting new people. Kids usually enjoy participating in this event. They can be a huge help in sorting items, moving furniture, and helping customers take items to their cars.

- O Invite an option of selling their old toys. Let them keep the money, if it is okay with their parents.

- O Encourage them to greet customers, answer questions, and be in charge of making change.

- O Set up a lemonade stand. Our granddaughter, Christine, made scones that were a huge hit at our sale. We sold and served coffee in the mugs that we had planned to sell. The customers were excited to keep the mugs. It was a great way to get rid of the 30 coffee mugs that had accumulated in our house over the years.

It was a great day of shared work!

Support with Technology

Ask for help with digital stuff. Kids are always pleased to assist as they generally have skills that exceed ours. Ben is a wiz at technology, and we are grateful for his assistance in solving our computer and television issues.

Top: Don and Tyler fix an outgrown bike to sell at the yard sale. Right: Everyone chipped in to help out at the yard sale.

Today is the last day of the garage sale, Christine is doing very well with her lemonade stand. Tyler and I have been helping carry things out for people. We're really hoping the table sells . . . Everything that doesn't sell will go to a charity. Overall, I think this weekend was a fun success.

Samuel, at 13

We each got a path in the woods named after us. Each grandchild would get a path cleaned and posted with our sign. We spent a lot of time running up and down these paths chasing each other.

Tyler, at 9

We have fun riding bikes at Grandma's house. Sometimes we go to the park and other times to the YMCA. The park has a path that goes around the two ponds and my brother and I race around them.

Ben, at 8

Treasured Traditions

6

A family is a group of people who are connected to each other through resilient bonding. Some family members are chosen through adoption or various other relationships. Family communities are strengthened by observing traditions and participating in rituals. Traditional festivities provide time to care for one another and enjoy that special time in each other's lives. The memories that we make with our families are priceless.

Planning Stress-free Holidays

Ahhhh, the holidays… that most wonderful time of year! There is something comforting and stabilizing about sharing the holidays with family. Usually, these days are filled with a mix of news, amazing food, and often a political debate started by a cantankerous relative. Ah yes, that one. Quick hint—try diversion. Invite that uncle to hold the baby or ask that cousin for assistance in setting up an activity. Keeping family members engaged and laughing may minimize debates and debacles.

Coordinating holiday planning can be a challenge. Since we are blessed with more than one child and several grandchildren, it is often a challenge to coordinate family events. Add to that mix the realization that the outlaws will have their own family traditions and customs. Initiate a discussion with your child about the holidays. Discuss expectations and brainstorm options if there are conflicting views.

A favorite holiday activity is creating gingerbread houses.

Laughing with grandparents provides the key to lock in memories and strengthen family bonds.

Options for Holiday Gatherings

⁂ Alternate holidays each year.

⁂ Decide on specific holidays that each family can host. For example: one family will always plan Hanukah and the other family host the 4th of July.

⁂ Host joint gatherings.

⁂ Include the other relatives in planning holiday events.

The holiday season after my first son was born presented a challenge; we made every effort to travel to both sets of grandparents on Christmas Day. It was exhausting trying to satisfy both sides of the family. I felt guilty and relieved when we finally decided to disrupt family expectations and begin to celebrate a new tradition of spending Christmas day in our own home. Remembering those hectic days of travel when our children were little made it easier to accept the changes in family traditions when we became grandparents. While I miss hosting this holiday at our home, we have enjoyed revised traditions as ways to celebrate with our families.

Getting to know the outlaws as friends can be one of the richest experiences of the grandparent journey. We now save seats for each other at school and sporting events. Sitting together provides moments of cheering and laughter as we delight in grandkid success and support their efforts. There is a united effort to comfort the child who misses a critical basket or gets injured in the heat of a soccer game. We often enjoy getting together afterwards at a nearby restaurant.

We are truly blessed that we have been able to share time with cherished "outlaws." One night at a grandchild event, I was given a surprise bag from daughter-in-law Julie's mom. It was a hot pad embroidered with my name. Every time I see that sweet gift, I think of her with gratitude for nurturing such a wonderful wife for my son.

> Having 12 grandchildren means sometimes their home gets messy, but they're always so happy to have everyone over and never worry about messes.
> Val, daughter-in-law

The 4th of July is a great time to celebrate with our extended families.

Traditions of Your Tribe

It is a blessing when we can celebrate holidays with our children and grandchildren. Our philosophy has been the more the merrier. We relish the vibrant energy that each relative brings to our holiday events.

If distance or schedules limit getting together, send seasonal cards. Stickers and small surprises (wands, cartoons, bookmarks) provide an unexpected bonus. Additional details for activities can be found online.

60

Holidays Throughout the Year

Below is a list of fun ideas to acknowledge and celebrate each holiday throughout the year. While some holidays are more elaborate than others, every holiday is a chance to make memories!

Valentine's Day

❋ Supply materials for the kids to make valentines for their parents. Extra valentines can be crafted to share with neighbors, nursing homes, military vets, or to the homeless shelter.

❋ Send valentines to each grandchild via snail mail. Include heart stickers.

❋ Learn how Valentine's Day came about.

❋ Send emoji graphics in an email or text to celebrate. (This idea can be used for any holiday.)

President's Day

❋ Visit a local history museum or Presedential Library. Visit a living history museum such as the Lincoln Home in Springfield, Illinois. These museums provide captivating experiences for all.

❋ Participate in a Presidential trivia contest. Search for and share amazing facts about world leaders.

❋ Recall and share stories of the President or other world leader who was in power when you were their age. I remember a girl in my grade school wearing a poodle skirt with the words, "I Like Ike" during the election of President Dwight Eisenhower.

St. Patrick's Day

❋ Create clues for a progressive scavenger hunt to find the pot of gold (gold coin candies).

❋ Share the science of rainbows.

❋ Paint rainbow pictures. Create a color wheel with paint, pastels, or crayons.

❋ Hunt for four leaf clovers. Press between two pieces of wax paper and store between the pages of a heavy book for a few weeks. Put the clover in a frame with the child's picture. You can also search for other unusual leaves to press.

Be My Valentine

Create your own valentines with crazy poetry variations on the theme: "Roses are Red, Violets are Blue...". Don't you know I am crazy about you?"

Brenda Elsagher, friend

Easter

Easter is one of our favorite holidays. Our large yard provides the ideal place for an outdoor egg hunt. In record time the 12 kids easily find the 400 hidden plastic eggs filled with coins or tiny silly items. Cheap green plastic buckets are dusted off each year for egg collecting. Years ago, the older kids established an annual tradition called "bucket head pictures." Those recycled buckets end up on their heads every year for our annual picture.

* Color and decorate eggs.

* Craft miniature Easter baskets out of recycled plastic food containers.

* Plan an egg hunt. Hide one that is a unique color. We hide a black egg every year that has a special coin. It is the highlight of the hunt to find that black egg.

My favorite thing to do is the egg hunt.

Faith, at 6   Emma, at 6

Clockwise from top left: Ben helped start the "bucket head" pictures; Hunting for Easter eggs; Our annual grandchildren fun photo day; Race to find all the eggs.

Patriotism—Gratitude for Country: Memorial Day, 4th of July, Veteran's Day

* Attend local parades. Bring empty bags for goodies that might be distributed from parade participants. Establish "rules" ahead of time with cautions about darting into the street to retrieve goodies. Check edible items before consumption.

* Marvel at the fireworks. Plan for the wait with snacks and games. Bring Glow-in-the-Dark bracelets and light-up balls for precelebratory entertainment.

* Attend celebrations in cities that provide interactive historic displays and exhibits. Mimi had a history teacher who sparked her interest in the city of Boston and the events that occurred in the early years of the United States. Because of that, she chose Boston as her 8th grade trip.

* Send a picture or a letter of thanks to the local Veteran's Administration.

* Lay flowers on the graves of loved ones for Memorial or Veteran's Day. Share stories about the contributions of family members who have served.

* Invite discussions with family members who have served.

Indigenous People's Day (*previously called* Columbus Day)

* Explore books about Native Americans. Discuss the culture of native tribes. Visit museums that highlight local history.

* Become explorers using a compass and paper map (no GPS) during a hike at a local or state park.

* Plan a survival day in the outdoors or go camping, hiking, and/or fishing to understand the challenges of early pioneers. The guideline is that food must be found in the wild. You can hide some nut bars in the bushes! This activity is best done with experienced adult naturalists.

Each 4th of July, Rockford, Illinois has spectacular fireworks. For many years we met on the Jefferson Street bridge with snacks and lawn chairs to enjoy the show.

Don, husband

GRANDMA HINT

Younger children can be traumatized by the loud noises and flashing lights of fireworks. Headphones or ear plugs might be helpful. Reviewing videos of fireworks and explaining that they are loud might help prepare kids for the experience.

Ghoulish Games

One of my favorite memories was a Halloween-themed party. We formed teams and set up games in 5 areas. Games included Flying Ghosts, Witches Brew, and Ghost Snot.

We baked cookies today and they are always so good. I had so much fun mixing the dough and decorating the cookies for Halloween.

Mimi, at 11

Halloween

❊ Carve pumpkins and toast the seeds.

❊ Enjoy local trick-or-treating events. While collecting Halloween candy, Samuel asked questions about life during the 1800s at our local living museum Midway Village in Rockford, Illinois.

❊ Give a small baggie with toothbrushes, sugar-free gum, pencils, gizmos and gadgets. Truthfully—this was not their favorite treat!

❊ Request pictures of them in their costumes if you will not see them in person.

❊ Create a haunted house together—provide old sheets, scary make up, and costumes so they can be ghostly and ghastly characters. Welcome guests (parents, neighbors) to be the "customers."

❊ Halloween provides a unique opportunity for creative writing.

Dressing up is our favorite thing to do, especially at Halloween. Faith can turn any day into a dress-up day! Left: Cloe loves Halloween so much she wrote a book about it!

Thanksgiving Day

Sunflower Burst by Samuel, at 13

❋ Gift a gratitude journal to your grandchildren. Encourage them to notice the laughter in their life and ask them to record what was funny. Invite them to write about what they are thankful for.

❋ Trace hands on paper and color these in as "handy" turkeys. Use as place cards for Thanksgiving dinner.

❋ Begin a round-robin gratitude dialog on Thanksgiving Day by inviting contributions from all who would like to share. Katie initiated this before one of our holiday meals and it was inspiring to hear from every family member.

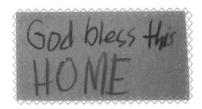

Giving Thanks

We are thankful for all of the people here today and for the love that they give to us.
Mimi, at 11

Andrew

Bowl of Fruit by Christine, at 13

Top: Samuel's sunflower art captures the joy of the holiday. Bottom left: Christine's bowl of fruit contributed to the colorful festivities. Right: All around the table for our Thanksgiving dinner—truly a treasured tradition! One year, Mimi said a powerful prayer before our family feast. In her prayer, she beautifully recognized the gifts of the people who care about her.

65

Holiday Delights

Winter Holidays (Hanukkah, Christmas, Kwanzaa, Epiphany, Las Posadas, Diwali)

✳ Gift a memory book of pictures from the previous year. This has been a favorite holiday gift and is a treasured reminder of how quickly the kids grow. The parents have loved these books.

✳ Garnish a gingerbread house with frostings and candies. Kits make it a lot easier, but graham crackers around boxes work well too. Remind the kids not to press too hard on the house (speaking from the experience of trying to put back together a collapsed house).

✳ Take a trip with your grandchild to a tree farm and select a holiday tree. Some families buy a tree that is potted for planting in the yard after the holiday.

✳ Invite your grandchild to sing or play holiday music for the family.

✳ Orchestrate a sing-along (the 12 days of Christmas was the perfect song for our family with each of the 12 grands enacting one of the 12 days).

✳ Enact a traditional play or find someone to recreate a character such as Saint Nicholas. We have had varying degrees of "success" with plays. I try to keep in mind that the process is more important than the product!

✳ One year we created tray favors for the nursing home where our grandson, Tyler, was working part time. He enjoyed delivering these to the residents and was able to tell them that they were made by his cousins.

✳ Investigate group games that have picture clues such as Santa Bingo so the younger children can play. Depending on the size of your party, you can form teams and offer silly prizes.

> ### Christmas Moments
>
> Today I baked cookies with Grandma. The last thing that we are making is homemade candy. It is taking forever to make. I can't wait for Christmas. The candy is finally done. I know we get to split the candy. I can't wait.
>
> Emma, at 12
>
> Today we ate lunch, played Santa Bingo and read our 2016 memory books. We got other stuff as well such as socks, spiky bouncy balls, and ornament letters.
>
> Samuel at 11

HAPPY new year

New Year's Eve

❋ Have a sleep over. Play games in pajamas and plan fun snack foods and sparkling nonalcoholic drinks. We have trouble staying up late and so we celebrate the New Year about 10:00 p.m. (after all, it is midnight somewhere!).

❋ Create party hats and, if you can stand the noise, provide horns and kazoos.

Katie's Journal
Happy New Year!

2015

Today Christine and Samuel and the rest of Peter's family came over. It was a lot of fun. We first ate lunch and then danced for a while.

Then we watched a movie. Then I got an early birthday present and Christine got a late Christmas present. They were matching New York Shirts. We want to go to New York when we grow up.

Katie, at 10

2016

I had fun today. We first made pancakes, then we went to the YMCA. We had a dance party there and then we played for a while. Then we got apple juice and had a balloon drop. But after that, everyone was hungry so we went to Steak and Shake. I had mini corn dogs and applesauce.

Then we went to the movie theater and watched the movie *SING*. It was a really good movie. Grandma taught me to play 5 Crowns. After that, Jan and John came over. We stuffed ourselves and played 7-UP and Apples to Apples. We missed the countdown, so we just yelled, "Happy New Year!" Tomorrow will be 2017.

Katie, at 11

Faith's interpretation
of Fireworks!

Faith, at 6

69

Passages and New Traditions

Grandparents can shape memories of transitional footsteps through time. Recognizing yearly growth with some of these symbols or events has become an eagerly anticipated custom in our family. Some of these ideas are familiar rites of passage and others have been initiated as new traditions in our family.

When Christine turned 13, we plastered signs everywhere in the house. She groaned and laughed when she found "Happy 13" signs in the bathrooms, inside the refrigerator, and on the front door.

❋ **Age 1: Growth Chart:** Start keeping track of their height with marks on a special wall in your house.

❋ **Age 2: Key Rings:** When the twins turned 2, we gave them their own set of keys. These were hung on a decorative rack in the toy area. Each subsequent child received a set. We saved old keys (cleaned with vinegar and baking soda) and put them on assorted rings. Ben and Tyler used these for starting racing cars and Faith stuffed hers into her purse for a pretend trip to the grocery store.

❋ **Age 3: Totes:** Fill a tote basket with crayons, colored paper, a lined notebook, stickers and envelopes. Write their name on it with a marker so they can haul it to a table and create their own "desk." The tote can hold their art materials as well as their stuff. Mimi spent hours with her tote. She especially liked sharpening her pencils with our electric pencil sharpener. She told me: "A really sharp pencil is important to do good work."

❋ **Age 4: Designated Path:** When a grandchild turns 4, Don clears a special trail in our woods and identifies the path with a namesake sign (see photos right). Four-year-olds love having their very own distinct outdoor space. If space is limited, a special garden spot can be selected and identified with their sign. Isaiah actually jumped up and down squealing in excitement when Grandpa opened his path. We use these trails as a starting point for the annual egg hunt.

❋ **Preschool or Kindergarten:** Keep a special folder with the artwork that they create. They love it when you frame their special works of art. Laminate their graduation certificate. Video tape their responses to questions about what made them laugh during the year.

❋ **Age 13: Crazy Sign Announcements:** Becoming a teenager is an exhilarating transition. Post wild, silly signs to proclaim this event and to encourage eyeball-rolling laughter.

Rites of Passage

I love how Mary Kay and Don encourage the kids to get outside! They made each
child a path outside in the wooded area behind their home. This has been such a neat
tradition and the kids love exploring their paths—each marked with their name.

Val, daughter-in-law

8th Grade Graduation Adventure: Grandparents/Grandkid Only

The 8th grade graduation trip has become an eagerly anticipated trip for our grandchildren. We invite them to choose a place in the country for travel with us. This week-long trip is the perfect opportunity to really get to know each individual grandchild.

This idea was generated and supported by my wonderful husband Don, who assists with every stage of each trip. Planning can begin with conversations as early as 5th grade. We encourage our grandkids to explore all types of ideas. For his trip, Andrew wanted to pan for gold, so we planned a trip to Yellowstone. His suitcase was filled with shovels and pans along with a few clothes. We spent time exploring many remote areas as he searched for the perfect spots to pan for gold.

Milestones

Don and Mary Kay started a tradition of taking each grandchild on a special vacation to celebrate their 8th grade graduation. The memories made on these trips are priceless!

Jennifer, daughter-in-law

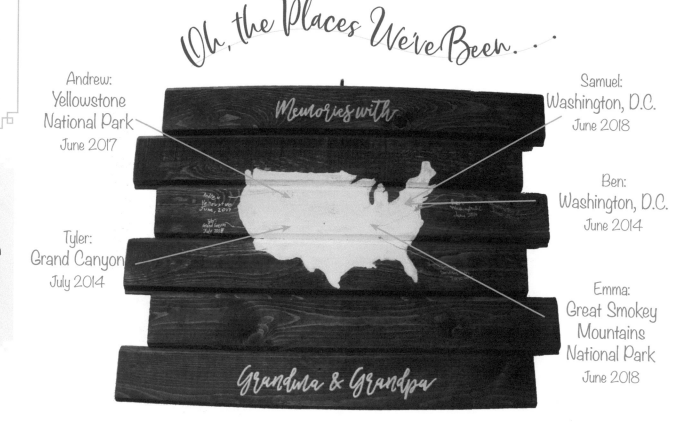

Oh, the Places We've Been...

Memories with

Andrew:
Yellowstone
National Park
June 2017

Samuel:
Washington, D.C.
June 2018

Ben:
Washington, D.C.
June 2014

Tyler:
Grand Canyon
July 2014

Emma:
Great Smokey
Mountains
National Park
June 2018

Grandma & Grandpa

Clockwise from top left: Tyler at the Grand Canyon; Emma with me at Dollywood; Andrew chose Yellowstone National Park so he could pan for gold. His suitcase was filled with a shovel, pans, and sluice, and a few clothes for hiking; Ben and me framing the Washington Monument.

Adventure Abounds!

My grandparents took me to the Smoky Mountains in Tennessee. One day, we went to Dolly Wood theme park. I was nervous to go on some of the rides, but being with my grandma and grandpa made it easier. In my mind I was thinking, "If my grandma and grandpa can do it, then so can I."

Emma, at 15

On my 8th grade trip, many funny things happened. Driving up to the top of the mountain, Grandma kept screaming because she was too close to the edge. Grandpa was giving us directions and we had no cell service, so I tried to find the map. I asked where the map was, and Grandpa replied that it was in the trunk.

Andrew, at 14

Driving at Sweet 16

Tyler was the first to get his driver's license. He is a very careful driver in spite of his first driving crisis on the Big Wheel at our house when he slid down the culvert and knocked his front tooth loose.

We were thrilled that one of Tyler's first trips in a car was to our house. Of course, his mom had him text her when he arrived safely here, and after a wonderful visit and a game of cards, I asked him to text me when he returned safely home. Not that we were worried or anything, but it is a blessing that new drivers can text after they safely arrive!

High School Graduation Scrap Book

Start a file for each grandchild when they are born. Over the years save their artwork, sporting/music programs and other mementoes to put in a graduation book. Include photos collected over the years. Add the cards or pictures they created for you. News clippings from the year they were born are an interesting addition. Their school colors provide memorable backgrounds.

Life Transitions: College, Jobs, Weddings

The grandparenting journey goes incredibly fast and before you know it, your grandbaby will be experiencing new opportunities and experiences. How can they already be in kindergarten, high school, or (OH, MY GOSH) in college? For one of the Duncan family reunions, my cousin, Mary Jo Duncan invited all of us to submit recipes from our grandmother and other relatives. She compiled all of them in the Duncan family cookbook with a wedding picture of my

The twins at their graduation. They inspired their younger sister and cousins to follow their dreams.

grandparents on the front cover. It is a sweet reminder of Aunt Rosemary when I make her banana bread and I can visualize Aunt Florence in her farm kitchen making her freezer jam. A recipe book is a cherished gift for a grandchild when they start living on their own.

Samuel, at 8

An Elephant never forgets, and I will never forget you!

Yesterday, Grandma picked me up from basketball and drove me to her house and we played games. The next day we woke up and Grandma told me it was a snow day and I got to stay all day with Grandpa and Grandma. We made monster pancakes and we went out at seven thirty in the morning and made a snowman and went sledding. Then I painted a plaque for grandma of a rooster. I ate Grandmas famous mac and cheese for lunch.

Steve, age 11

At Cloe's request, 11-year-old Christine baked her a cat cake for her birthday.

GRANDMA HINT

When roughhousing with grandkids (we "let" them win), we communicate confidence and teach them that winning is not everything. Our rule of thumb is to allow the cousins to roughhouse with each other until someone gets hurt. When they initiate rough and tumble activities, I often insist that hey go outside or to the playroom area.

Make Way for Cousins

If you are blessed to have several grandchildren, make every effort to get cousins together. This time together can nurture those special cousin bonds. Any of the activities in this book are great for cousin get-togethers, but often they just enjoy free play and creating their own imaginative activities.

✳ Ben and Andrew took apart and rebuilt a scooter so they could do even crazier tricks on it. An 8-year-old neighbor warned that was a dangerous activity. Andrew said, "Yep—we do crazy things in this family! That's how we roll." This story was laughingly told by a cousin afterwards, and to my knowledge no one was hurt. Sometimes it is better not to know…

✳ The grandkids often share ideas of what would be fun to do with their cousins. We have had suggestions for bike rides, hiking trips, games, and parties. Sometimes we go to county fairs or museums. We have invited some of the cousins to join us at a sporting event to cheer another cousin. Emma was pleased when several of her cousins came to cheer at her volleyball game.

✳ By the age of 11, Christine had won several 4-H awards in cake decorating. She was honored when her cousin, Cloe, asked her to make a cat birthday cake for her 9th birthday party. Christine came over and we enjoyed making and decorating the cake and cupcakes for Cloe's party.

✳ Laughter is what we are after. When you encourage your grandchildren to spend time with each other it will have a profound impact on their life and on yours. A loving interactive relationship is critically important for kids who spend a vast amount of time communicating with others through their devices. Having playful fun with family members will be long remembered. Shared laughter builds trust.

✳ Playful roughhousing is an integral part of leadership development and negotiation skills according to Anthony T. DeBenedet and Lawrence J. Cohen in their book, *The Art of Roughhousing*. Rough and tumble play encourages self-confidence, fairness, and empathy. It encourages giving up power and negotiating friendship. Playful roughhousing prevents hurtful behavior and helps with the development of social awareness and cooperation.

Grandma and Grandpa's House…

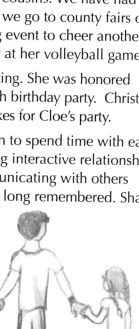

Where Cousins become best friends

Cousins sketch by Katie, at 14.

Cousins Bonding!

RENT ME

2100

My grandma taught us that cousins should have good relationships with each other. She set times for me to bond with my girl cousins, and we all have become good friends. Even though we have our differences, we still can get together and have a good time. I'm always glad to know that my gal pals got my back.

Katie, at 14

The Big Fish

By Christine, at 12

When the cousins and I were little we fought over a stuffed fish. We would play by seeing who could get the fish. The cousins would tackle each other in order to "win." Whoever actually got the fish would laugh at the other "losers" and they would say, " Ha, ha, I got the fish and you don't."

Then in response we would gang up on that person and do a group tackle, where we would eventually be a large heap on the floor. We were all so close, like brothers and sisters. Now that fish is well retired, and we don't fight over it anymore, but I know the cousins and I will always remember that fish and the story that goes with it.

Fish art by Steve, at 12

Fish art by Isaiah, at 6

79

It's always great to feel supported. Having my grandparents there to watch my matches was always special to me because I knew they were taking an interest in what was important to me. When the whole cheering squad was there I felt all the love radiating from the crowd. Fortunately my grandma never started the wave like she threatened. Love them all a ton!

Katie, at 15
Background art by Isaiah, at 7

80

The Superpowers of Grandparents

7

Your superpower is the special relationship that you have with your grandchild. It is difficult to describe the unique quality of this bond. Grandparents have the power to let their grandchild experience the blessing of unconditional love. This is not just a quiet acceptance of who they are, but it can often be a loud and enthusiastic proclamation of their special abilities and talents. Grandparents are not afraid to share (brag) about their grandchildren. Grandchildren usually savor this unabashed adoration of unconditional love.

There are a lot of jokes about how lenient grandparents can be. It is generally understood that enthralled grandparents will let their grandkids do whatever they want. *Grandparents—so easy to operate, even a child can do it.*

Many kids know that on the rare occasion that Grandma says "no," Grandpa can be an easy "yes." However, there will be times when you both need to say "no." The difficult moments are often when you can make the most significant impact on their lives. Modeling and teaching self-control is a valued measure of grandparenting.

Along with unconditional love, grandparents possess the wisdom to provide guidance for emotional regulation. Each loving interaction builds upon those special bonds. Sharing heritage and family connections can provide a strong sense of purpose that is essential to mental health. And of course, playful learning is the best way to build fundamental life skills that reduce stress and contribute to healthy living.

"I will always love you, no matter what you might say or do."

Not all heroes wear capes. Some heroes are disguised as grandparents.

Reminder: The 4 Benefits of Humor

The research on the psychology of humor suggests that there are numerous benefits for infusing humor into difficult situations. The emotional bonds of trust, hope, optimism, and love are the foundation of a laughter-filled relationship.

1. Trust:

Fun and laughter are indicators of a high level of trust within a healthy relationship.

2. Hope:

Humor is the sign of positivity within individuals and organizations. Humor expresses the hope that we can survive tragedy, difficulty, and change and not only survive, but thrive.

3. Optimism:

The energy of humor reflects a confident spirit. Humor practice and a focus on positivity can decrease stress and depression.

4. Love:

When exploring close relationships, the number one characteristic mentioned as vital is a sense of humor. Laughter is a universal connection that builds rapport and supports a loving relationship.

Morrison 2008

A Very Special Love

If you have several grandchildren, there will be unique interpersonal interactions with each of them. Some may want to be assured of your special love for them.

At age 5, Isaiah asked me, "Who is your favorite grandchild?" How could I let him know that his spirit was a magical part of my life that no one else could ever fill? I responded that "each of you has a special place in my heart." I assured him that his was a very special spot that was just especially for him.

Discipline

It is hard to believe, but your incredible grandchild may misbehave or be disruptive at times.

That is when grandparent superpower skills come to the rescue. Make sure all (including parents) agree on some basic discipline guidelines. Of course, when the parents are present, they make the decisions. Discuss any differences of opinion but do follow their recommendations when they leave you with their precious child.

There has been controversy about the use of physical force over the years. Many of us grew up in a home where paddling was an accepted form of punishment. While discipline is absolutely necessary, the research on the negative consequences of spanking is clear. The use of physical force of any kind is unacceptable, unless you need to restrain a child who is hurting himself or another person.

Haim Ginott is a well-known child psychologist, who relays his famous story about the inherent contradictions of corporal punishment:

A mother is working in the kitchen quickly trying to cook dinner. Her 5-year-old son and his 3-year-old brother are playing on the floor nearby. The two boys start fighting over a toy and the older boy delivers a punch to the head of his younger sibling. Seeing this, the mother stops cooking and grabs the older boy by the arm. She delivers a strong swat to his bottom and says, "You should never hit someone smaller than you."

When a child hits a child,
        we call it aggression.
When a child hits an adult,
        we call it hostility.
When an adult hits an adult,
        we call it assault.
When an adult hits a child,
        we call it "discipline."

—Haim G. Ginott

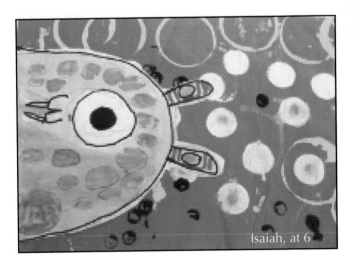

Isaiah, at 6

LOL MAGIC

Is It Age Appropriate?

When faced with frequent meltdowns or self-control issues, it is helpful to review information about age-related expectations.

It is often reassuring to learn that a challenging behavior is normal for a child of that age, and to discover strategies that are age appropriate.

. . . .

GRANDMA HINT

Breathing like a fish and blowing bubbles is a fun strategy for finding self-control and to calm young children.

83

Discipline: A Superpower

Prevention

Keeping kids active and engaged is the best way to avoid inappropriate behavior. There are numerous recommendations in this book to plan ahead for playful, laughter-filled visits. Even if you have well-thought out plans, know that there may be a few hiccups, but the best strategy is to have several back-up plans.

No, but . . .

When you have to say "NO,"
follow it up by saying
"but I have a crazy surprise
for you!"

Katie getting into the Surprise Drawer—the drawer where I keep lots of stuff for them to do.

Above and bottom right: Provide a tote for each child so they can set up their own "office."

84

Boundaries and Consequences

Children have trust in you and feel more secure when they know the "rules." They will be reassured when they know their boundaries. Unconditional love includes making sure the child understands that you will keep him/her safe and not allow hurtful behavior.

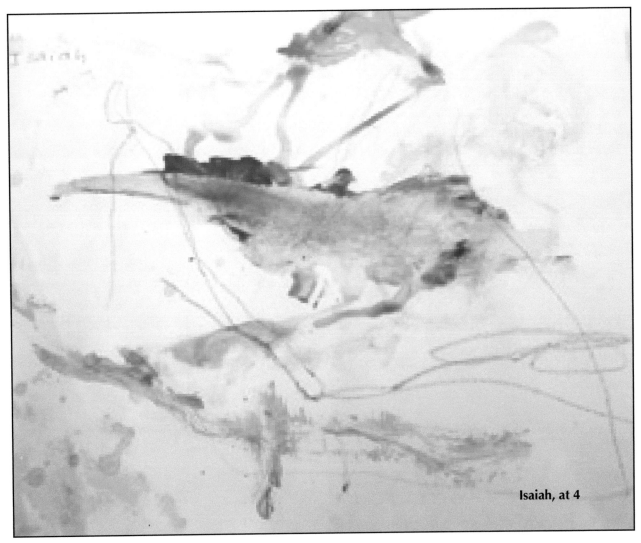

Isaiah, at 4

Defining boundaries are important for building trust.

Isolation

It is common for young children to hit or bite when they are upset or frustrated. Calmly state that they must stop the behavior and they need to go to a quiet place (crib/time-out chair) until they calm down. When they are composed, have a discussion with them. Repeat several times, if necessary, that it is ok to be angry, but they can never hurt anyone else.

If they feel like biting, they can bite an apple, but not others. If they feel like hitting, suggest they try hitting a punching bag or large ball. Let them know that they can express their frustration but can never hurt another person.

Animals are often the light for children when the world seems dark.

Katie remembers being invited to go outside to "think."

Steve, at 10

Time-out can be effective with some children. Use one minute for each age of the child (5 minutes for a 5-year-old).

Once I told my son that I was counting on him (for appropriate behavior) and he said, "No! Don't Count on Me." He thought I was going to give him the "Count of 3," which was the warning before time out.

Consequences should fit the age of the child. It is often effective to ask them what they think their consequences should be. This trust in their abilities often leads to their suggestions for consequences that are more severe than what you were considering.

Always listen carefully to whatever your grandchildren tell you. Reflect on their feelings about what they told you-even if it is little stuff. When they get older, they will confide the big stuff.

Cloe, at 11

87

Private Conversations

If a child is being disruptive or having a tantrum, quietly invite that child for a private conversation with you in another part of the house. Identify the behavior and give them the chance to correct it. Remind them of the consequences if the disruption continues. Examples would be isolation or taking away electronic devices. A private conversation is also a time to let them know you are optimistic about their ability to behave appropriately. Sometimes their disruptive behavior is a way to get attention and the private conversation can provide a magical turnaround.

Re-directing

Sometimes the best strategy for minor misbehavior is to offer another option for play and fun. Calmly state that they must stop the behavior and they will need to go to a quiet place until they are ready to join the family again. Suggest they read or listen to music. When they are composed, have a discussion with them. Convey your optimism that they can change their behavior.

Some additional options for redirecting including providing manipulative materials such as Playdoh, pipe cleaners, or fingerpaint.

Top right: Take a disruptive child to a private place to offer them a sense of calm and the attention they might need.
Bottom: Isaiah "cooking" with Play-Doh®. Right page clockwise: Christine runs off excess energy; Katie creates art with pipe-cleaners; Samuel enjoys a tub of dry macaroni (less messy than sand); Isaiah learns to blow bubbles.

Affirmations

Look for any positive effort or behavior, recognize, and verbalize it. If you suggest taking a deep breath and they do so, be sure to mention that you appreciate their effort to calm their mind. You are teaching invaluable skills for emotional regulation when you valuate their efforts. It is a message expressing hope that they can survive and thrive in difficult situations. Mediation and relaxing exercises are also ways to affirm their ability to control their behavior.

Ask grandchildren to assist with chores. They will enjoy helping you.

President Joe Biden says he has a strict rule about his phone: No matter what's happening, he always answers a call from one of his grandchildren.

Source: CNN

Clockwise from top left: Katie helps fill the bird feeders, and delights in watching the birds enjoy her hard work; Emma helps in the kitchen; Tyler shows off the tables he sanded for us; Cloe is a big help picking garden vegetables for our salad.

Confidence and Consequences

You may have several children at your home at the same time. These might be siblings, cousins, or friends. Squabbles can occur for a variety of reasons. When they do occur, have confidence in their abilities and trust them to work it out by encouraging them to resolve the issue without you.

It is helpful to ask a leading question: "How are you going to resolve this?" This can be followed by a statement: "I know that the two (three) of you can figure this out." It can be effective to walk away (showing confidence in their ability to solve the problem.) They usually prefer to be with each other, but if they need some alone time, put them in separate "boring" rooms without electronic devices. Let them know they can be together again after they are ready to resolve their differences.

If kids are physically hurting each other, separate and isolate them until they are calmer. Talk to them about what they could have done differently. If they are old enough, ask them to write about the issue, and how they could change their behavior. Remind them that hitting is not allowed and the next time it occurs, name a consequence. The following consequences have been effective with children over 5 years old:

- No electronic devices for 2 hours
- Request they write about how they will react differently the next time
- Take away a privilege (something fun that was going to happen)

Redirecting works for groups, too. "Let's try these new paint pens."

Challenge them to race to a tree and back.

Junior high kids may pretend they don't care what you have to say, but they can't help but listen.

I am so glad when I get to spend time at Grandma's house. She does her best to understand me, which can be hard as I get older. I am blessed to have her in my life.

Katie, at 14

Guidance for Tweens and Teens

There may be moments with pre-teens and teens, especially when they are with their friends, that they are uncomfortable doing anything "embarrassing." Ah, the angst of teenage years can be a challenge for everyone. Your grand may be immersed in a world that is confusing and scary. Your role as a "cool" grandparent may change overnight. There may be fewer hugs and less time together. Explore various ways to interact with your pre-teens and teens.

Humor

Acknowledge changes that are taking place in your relationship with laughter and good humor. Social media can be a great tool. Text funny memes or goofy graphics to celebrate an ordinary day. Recently, I sent each teen grandchild a dancing chicken and with this note: "Hope you have a dancing chicken kind of day." I also mentioned that I could see the eyerolls from my house. Emoji eyerolls are invaluable for these kinds of exchanges. Expect them to send "eye rolls" back to you.

Katie, at 15

Confidentiality

They may confide in you about situations they are experiencing with bullying or questions about addictions or suicide. Keep what they tell you as a confidential sacred trust unless you are worried about their health or safety. Then let them know that you are concerned and must share it with their parents. If it is feasible, a better option is to encourage them to share the information with their parents. Assure them you will be there to support them.

The teen years are an opportune time to listen to concerns and doubts. One granddaughter asked what she should do about some challenges with friends. She asked for advice. She was a bit frustrated when I did not actually give advice but asked her to come up with suggestions on how she could handle it on her own. I let her know that what might work for me, might not be the best solution for her. I emphasized that it was important for her to make her own decisions so she would feel comfortable with the choices she made.

Teenagers: *Creative, Capable, and Collaborative!*

Invite your teen to help plan and participate family events.

I put my GoPro up in bird nests and videotaped them growing up.

Steve, at 13

Clockwise from top left: Christine and Emma plan the family event for Christine's holiday play; Samuel, Katie, and Christine are each team captains for the Scavenger Hunt; Katie and Emma organize the Christmas gift exchange; Christine and Samuel traveled with us to support Katie at her middle school play (inset).

Grandparents can be the calm
during life's storms.

Samuel, at 13

94

The Power of Comfort and Love During and After the Storm

When there are meltdowns and/or even mental health issues while in your care, you need to assure the child that it is going to be okay and that they are okay. Offer calming reassurance and optimism—some phrases to remember:

- *Take your time.*
- *It's okay.*
- *No worries.*
- *Take deep breaths.*
- *It's gonna be all right.*
- *I love you—always!*

They may act like they are not listening, but they will appreciate calm interventions.

Always offer hugs and support: Enjoy the hugs!

Young people can be a huge support to each other.

A Light in the Darkness

Indeed, a calming presence is a much-needed gift in times of chaos and confusion, one that's willing to say, "It's okay," "I'm with you," "It'll all be fine."

These simple yet powerful words not only calm big emotions but assure children, and adults for that matter, that they are safe right now. All is good in this present moment, which allows the present-oriented heart to rest and remain open and the child to continue being saturated in the joys and wonders of timelessness.

—Vince Gowmon
Healing for a New World

Be a Calming Presence

Knowing your grandchild's personality, offer ideas on ways for them to de-stress.

❋ Invite them to go for a walk with you or to participate in an energizing physical activity.

❋ Try meditation or mindful activities.

❋ Encourage them to participate in a quiet, reflective time with time for reading, music, or art to be mindful and reenergize.

- Draw or color.

- Ride a bike or practice the hula hoop.

- Take a soothing bath.

- Listen to a favorite band.

- Immerse in a creative outlet.

Katie, at 13

The emotional bonds of trust, hope, optimism, and love are the foundation of a laughter-filled relationship. Grandparents have a unique opportunity to use their superpowers to nurture these qualities with their grandchildren, especially in difficult or challenging situations.

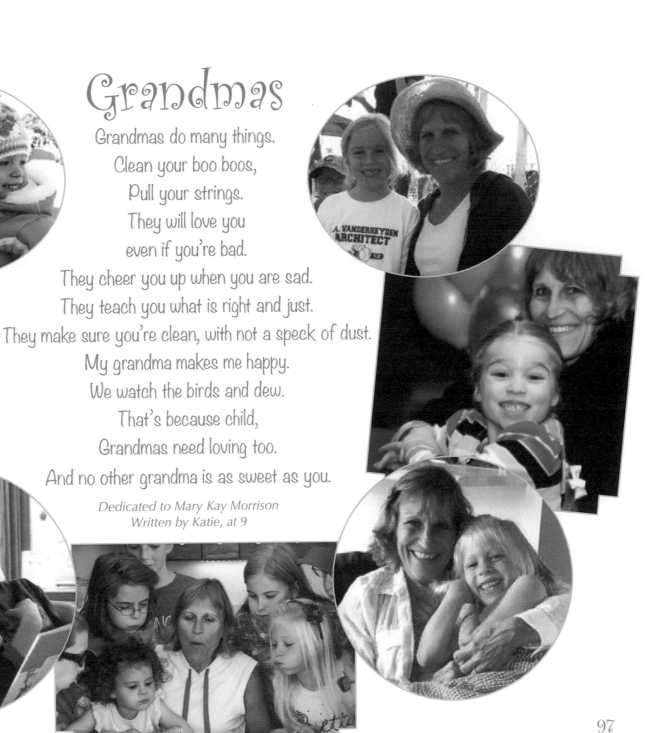

Grandmas

Grandmas do many things.
Clean your boo boos,
Pull your strings.
They will love you
even if you're bad.
They cheer you up when you are sad.
They teach you what is right and just.
They make sure you're clean, with not a speck of dust.
My grandma makes me happy.
We watch the birds and dew.
That's because child,
Grandmas need loving too.
And no other grandma is as sweet as you.

Dedicated to Mary Kay Morrison
Written by Katie, at 9

97

Swinging makes me happy. I like seeing how high I can go and enjoying the nice view from the top!

Christine, at 13

The Tough Stuff is Fertile Ground for Humor

8

You are that mighty oak! In a nutshell, humor is the fundamental and integral core of our cognitive emotional growth. The fertile ground of trust and the elements of nurturing relationships are required for seeds to take root. How can grandparents nourish the little nuts that are searching for the ground in which humor can flourish? The survival of the oak is a story of laughing with the winds of change and being optimistic during the storms of life.

As you adjust to the change in dynamics with this treasured addition to your family, be mindful that you have survived a lot in life. This survival strength will be a vital source of grounding for your little "nut."

Today's mighty oak is just yesterday's nut that held its ground.

—David Icke

Playful Aging

The mix of love and laughter are especially important as you embrace new realities in your own life. There are often factors beyond your control that may impact or limit your interactions with your grandchild. It takes an exceptionally optimistic mindset to recognize, prepare for and accept difficult challenges. As you probably know, laughter is a key contributor to living longer.

The Mayo Clinic website recommends laughter as a therapeutic strategy for coping with stress and depression. Think about how you played as a child and include more playfulness in your life. Be playful with your grandchild. It will benefit both of you immeasurably. Play is an effective trigger for laughter.

Cloe, at 8

Ben's first attempt at writing a note to
Grandpa (age 5). These kinds of notes
of love from grandchildren reduce stress
and bring joy.

Survive and Thrive

While fun never asks how old you are, you may recognize that you do not have the same vitality that you had several years ago. There may be some physical and/or mental limitations that limit your time and energy. As we discussed in Chapter 2, self-care is extremely important.

Find Time for Yourself

My son was severally burned in an accident about two weeks after moving into their new home. We gladly packed up the four kids and brought them to live with us during his healing. We have many wonderful memories of our time together. We made sure they got to school and to the hospital to visit their dad. This period was a reality check for me, as I had forgotten how much time and energy it takes just to do the cooking and laundry for four kids.

After a week of full-time grandparenting, I asked the kids to get ready for bed. Instead, there were several minutes of bickering about who had to get a bath first. I found myself yelling at all of them to get moving. The two younger ones burst into tears and ran to the bathroom crying, and the older ones looked like they had seen a ghost. I realized the they had not heard me get upset before. I had always been a "fun" grandma. I apologized as I tucked them into bed. Then the guilt set in. I was upset with myself for losing my temper.

In reflection afterward, I recognized that we were all exhausted and they had been through several life-changing events including a new home, new school, and a loved one in the hospital.

Take time to play. You are never too old. It is invigorating to
create snow angels.

Swinging can be very soothing.

A ride on a merry-go-round will help you forget some of the ups and downs of life.

There is no such thing as a perfect parent.

There is no such thing as a perfect grandparent.

Forgive yourself.

Expect bloopers.

Find a way to laugh afterwards.

I had a renewed appreciation for my son and his wife. The good news was that he completely healed, and this tragedy bonded us even more closely as a family. We are eternally grateful for the blessing of his health and for the precious time we were able to spend with their kids.

Most of us experience unexpected change, suffering and loss in our lives. As we are able to find the humor in a situation, we can begin to heal and move ahead. Difficult experiences, if met with hope and optimism can generate remarkable growth opportunities. In fact, humor frequently emerges from the down-side of our lives.

Inner peace comes when we are able to find humor in our painful experiences.

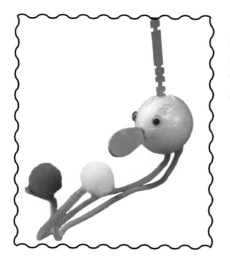

Emma, at 6, created a magic animal with pipe cleaners and other fun materials.

Grandchild Quiet Time

Screaming babies can be stressful. If you have an upset baby that cannot be comforted, you may need to put in her in the crib for a short time and insert ear plugs. If the child is old enough, let them know you need some rest. Take the time you need to restore your balance. Provide activities that they can do on their own while you re-energize with a cup of hot tea.

❋ Put on an audio book.

❋ Provide soothing music.

❋ Provide blocks or manipulative toys.

❋ Encourage outside play in an enclosed deck or safe area.

❋ Get out a new toy or magazine (keep some wrapped in the closet).

❋ Introduce the **Surprise Jar**

Write several suggestions on paper and put into a jar that you have prepared ahead of time for this grandchild surprise activity. They get to choose and read the "surprise" activity. The deal is that if they want to pick and read a slip from the jar, they need to agree that they will do whatever the surprise slip says.

Possible options:

• Draw a picture for your parents or for another relative.

• Read a book:
  ▪ in a tent with a flashlight (indoors—put a blanket over a table)
  ▪ outside in a swing
  ▪ on a blanket in the grass

• Assemble a puzzle.

• Create a magic animal with colorful pipe cleaners

• Play with Legos or blocks

Sisters Katie and Cloe supported each other during the pandemic (Cloe, at 13, sketched this picture).

Christine picked a slip from the Surprise Jar that read: "Feed the Birds."

102

When I see my sleeping grandchildren, I am grateful to the angels that watch over them as they play at my house.

SWEET DREAMS LOADING...

We spent many hours reading in the Book Nook. Often, these quiet moments ended with a nap. I sometimes had to call Don to help get me up and out of the chair without waking the little ones.

GRANDMA HINT

Grandchildren can be exhausting. Getting enough sleep is vital for all of you.

A good laugh and a long sleep are the two best cures for anything.

Irish Proverb

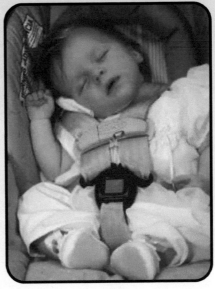

Katie, at 14

104

Trauma and Mental Health Challenges

There may be family members coping with trauma or mental health challenges. When you have concerns about your own health or about the well-being and safety of your child or grandchild, you may need to make painful decisions about your involvement in their lives. Some grandparents may worry that they will be denied access to grandchild visits. In many places, grandparents have legal rights. Each circumstance is different, but it is helpful to search for the resources and support groups that can provide assistance.

The trauma might be hidden, and grandparents can help unmask the challenges and provide support.

Unfortunately, situations such as the one described below are more common than we would like to think. Grandparents help fill many roles and their importance cannot be overstated.

> Our grandchildren, ages 6 and 7, have a mother who is an alcoholic and has been diagnosed with a mental health issue. We live an hour away and do everything we can to be there for them. We've driven an hour to see our granddaughter's half hour gymnastics class or to watch our grandson's soccer game. When we are together, we give them special attention, so they experience happiness, laughter, and love. Playing games, doing puzzles, and coloring are on the their list of favorite activities, which gives us a chance to have conversations with them, which they crave. We support our son's efforts to provide therapy for these kids. Even though they confide in us, as they get older, they will need another "ear."
>
> —*An Anonymous Friend*

Family dysfunction rolls down from generation to generation, like a fire in the woods, taking down everything in its path until one person in one generation has the courage to turn and face the flames.

That person brings peace to their ancestors and spares the children that follow.

— *Terry Real*

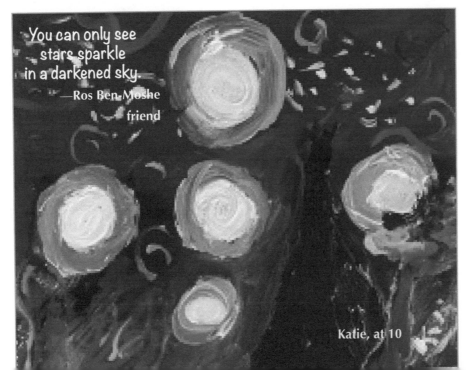

You can only see stars sparkle in a darkened sky.
—Ros Ben-Moshe
friend

Katie, at 10

105

Laughter for Special Needs

Some families have kids or family members with special educational needs or other disabilities.

❋ Honor the unique abilities of these children and their family members. Include them in as many activities as possible.

❋ Explore ways to adapt for special needs. Adaptive technology may simplify and enhance communication.

❋ Invite other family members to brainstorm ways to include everyone in activities and games. Often the person with the disability will offer the best suggestions.

❋ Recognize and focus on talents: Make it a habit to notice their aptitudes. We grow from our strengths—not by focusing on limitations. Recognize their abilities and foster them. Often art or music can be an optimal way to provide flourishing opportunities for kids that have challenges.

Kids with attention deficit hyperactivity disorder, autism, and anxiety benefit from kinesthetic activities.

Fidget toys can actually help with mental processing while doing school work. A rainbow popper is popular for kids of all ages.

Community resources can provide invaluable assistance. Scout out mental health services. Locate playgrounds that include equipment for folks with physical challenges. Search for supportive resources for kids with special needs.

let life surprise you

Samuel, at 8

Slime is a great stress relieving activity.

106

Cloe, at 8

Play... Play... Play!

Play triggers laughter.

All kids and adults benefit from play, and those who are disabled have an even greater need for play and laughter in their lives.

Humor generates trust and can facilitate a reduction in tension, fear and anger. It takes effort to assist others in seeing the "humor" in difficult situations. Laughter can nurture communication and ease tense situations. Exaggeration, puns, and self-deprecating humor are tools of the trade. When we are able to use reframing humor (example: the ridiculous or exaggeration), it can facilitate a shift in focus and enable creative thinking. Laughter can quickly dispel tension and increase the capacity for positive interaction.

Find the Funny!

Humor is not about being funny, it is about SEEING Funny!

—Karyn Buxman
neurohumorist, friend

Music can be a fun motivator. Here Samuel and Christine dance to lively piano music.

My brother Richard has such a hearty, contagious laugh. He was delighted to give each of the twins a guitar from his Mexico trip.

Don always finds ways to laugh with the grandkids—usually by creating silly puns or putting on red noses.

Create a List of Happiness Strategies

After a discussion with a grandchild about the challenges in her life, I encouraged her to create a list of ideas on how she might find ways to feel better. It tickles me that many of these strategies are beneficial for me as well. Unfortunately, I no longer fit under my bed.

Try These Happiness Strategies

❋ Think of funny things or funny names— try to make myself laugh
❋ Punch a pillow
❋ Hug or hold a cute stuffed animal
❋ Go in the backyard to find bugs
❋ Squeeze a ball
❋ Sing
❋ Go under the bed with animals— close your eyes and think happy thoughts
❋ Pet my cat
❋ Get a hot bath
❋ Breathe big breaths
❋ Listen to mindful tapes.
❋ Give Mommy, Daddy, or Grandma a big hug and kiss
❋ Ask for a backrub
❋ Sit down and read a book
❋ Sketch nature

Right top: In the backyard with Katie looking for butterflies and bugs. Bottom: Katie reflecting on what makes her feel better.

Katie, at 15

109

Create a Survival Game: *It Could Have Been Worse*

Laughter is an indicator of a high level of trust within relationships. When we can find laughter in a situation, we know we are able to cope.

Moving is always a challenge. We were thrilled that our son and his wife had finally found a wonderful home for their family of four kids. On moving day, my husband and I were the first to arrive at their new home with two cars jam-packed with stuff. Christine had been buckled in the seats amid the baskets and lamps. After we arrived, we waited for an endless amount of time. She came up with a game while we waited and wrote this article that describes how we were able to find some laughter in the craziness of the day. By the time the other movers arrived with a key, we had been laughing so hard that we almost had tears running down our legs. Thank heavens for the porta potty in the forest preserve and for the ability of this 12 year old to find the funny!

And YES, the laughter is what we will remember.

The rain does not stop Christine and Isaiah from having fun.

You can always find ways to be cheerful when things don't go your way.

Christine, at 12

C.H 2/16

110

It Could Have Been Worse

By Christine, at 12

We were moving to our new house the day after the closing. I had slept over at Grandma's house the night before along with Isaiah and Faith. We dropped them off at school that morning and headed over to the new house. My dad had texted us the code to the garage so we could get in. Dad was getting the U-Haul and Samuel was with Grandpa Heinisch, to pick up some things. Grandma and I pulled into the driveway of our new house and Grandpa was already there. It turned out that the garage door code just didn't work. Great.

We needed the key. We tried calling Samuel and he didn't pick up. Then we tried calling Grandpa Heinisch with the same results. We then called Dad who answered, saying that they were at the Deck's getting table and chairs. So, we called Grandpa Deck, no answer. And did I mention it was pouring out?!! We were stuck in the car for an hour trying to get a hold of someone.

Then Grandma and I had to go to the bathroom, Wow terrible timing. So, we drove down to a forest preserve and on the way there we thought we spotted grandpa's truck. So, we went back to the house. You guessed it, that wasn't their truck! So back we went to go to the bathroom and on the way, I thought of a game that cheered us up.

I called it "It could have been worse. Yep, it pretty much means what it says. I said, "Well it could have been worse if there wasn't a potty nearby." "Yes, or we could have peed our pants already," Grandma replied. We kept thinking of thing that could have been worse than they already were. By the time we got to the forest preserve we were laughing. The river was nearby, and Grandma said, "Hey, just leave the bathroom door open and we can have a wonderful view of the river." I was unwilling to do that!

We came back to the house and still no sign of anyone. We called everyone at least five times. The rain had stopped pouring, so we got out and tried to find another way in. I tried to pick the lock and that was also not a success. Eventually both trucks arrived, and we got in. In total it was about two hours of waiting for them. It turned out fine though. In all we learned two things: That You can always find ways to be cheerful when things don't go your way. And our new house is the most secure, locked house in the world!!"

Let go of what you cannot control. Recognize that there may be difficult moments.

Breathe!

No matter how cold and wet my soccer games can be, I always have a great time when my family is there with me. I'll never forget when my grandparents came to one of my games in the pouring rain on a really cold day. We've always said that they won the Grandparents of the Year Award on that day.

Samuel, at 16

Electronic Devices and the Neuroscience of Play 9

Recently I was trying to figure out how to create passwords that I might actually remember. It occurred to me that our grandchildren have always been connected to electronics. As infants, baby monitors kept a constant check on breathing and their movements creating digital natives (kids who have always lived with electronic devices.) Most children are exposed to digital devices at a young age. Our grandchildren are probably somewhat oblivious to technology since it has always been an integral part of their lives.

The good old days have been zapped by technology. Would we really want to return to days before cell phones? Mind-boggling technological changes make our lives easier but also more challenging. Our cell phones not only allow us to stay in touch with family and friends, they give us instant access in emergencies. A simple click will immediately give us verbal directions to appointments and the ability to order food on-line for quick delivery. They also do crazy things like invite us to choose a ring-tone that seems to be the same one as every other person in the grocery store.

The benefits of technology are a mixed blessing. Our grandkids will certainly not know what fun it is to refold one of those huge car paper maps or be tied to a phone with a stretchy cord attached to the wall. But they will know the joy of texting with their grandparents and we will know the joy of digital conversations with them.

In the good old days we did not have the challenges that confront kids today. Social media, school shootings, and self-driving cars were not part of our childhood. Bullying was done on the school playground, not in our bedrooms when we were trying to go to sleep. Our digital devices were calculators, and a mouse was a rodent that we trapped if found in our garage.

Grandparents can encourage playtime as a healthy break from device time.

Hooked on Electronic Devices

Emerging research indicates that too much time on electronic devices can actually lead to physical and mental health challenges. It is easy to get hooked on our devices. Every ping on a phone is an instant distraction. I find myself grabbing my phone to see who has just texted me. My twitter account constantly feeds me *Breaking News*.

I can only imagine the challenges of parents who are getting messages from work in the evening—long after their regular workday. Many parents are so stressed in their own lives that educational programs on digital devices are seen as a child-care option. And these kids are oblivious to the constant device distractions.

From a young age, kids are spending an enormous amount of time on electronics leading to significant concerns. Mayo Clinic recommends that children under the age of 24 months have little or no time on devices, except for video chatting. For children from 2 to 5 screen time should be limited to one hour a day of high quality programs.

What does too much screen time do to kids brains?

Research indicates an increasing concern about the impact of technology on our health and well-being. Early data from a landmark National Institutes of Health (NIH) study that began in 2018 indicate that children who spent more than two hours a day on screen-time activities scored lower on language and thinking tests, and some children with more than seven hours a day of screen time experienced thinning of the brain's cortex, the area of the brain related to critical thinking and reasoning. Excessive use of electronic devices has been linked to:

- Less tolerance, increased anger

- Depression and anxiety

- Digital eye strain

- Sleep disturbances

- Relationship problems

- Obesity

- Loss of playtime

Mouse droppings!

Play involves various centers of perception and cognition in the entire brain. Limiting play disrupts brain maturation. As our children spend more and more time on devices, they are deprived of the vital opportunities that play provides for brain growth.

Unplug the Kids

The laughter is what we are after. Shared laughter will not occur when kids are on their devices. I recommend little or no time on electronic devices when visiting grandparents (unless the child is older than 8 and staying for an extended length of time.)

If they know that you will have exciting activities and fun surprises planned, they will probably be more accepting of a strict time limit on cell phones during their visits.

Decline of Play and Rise of Mental Illness

Stress in our society is at an all-time high. Many parents struggle with work/family balance. There are significant numbers of kids who are diagnosed with depression, attention issues, and trauma-induced anxiety.

In his book *Freedom to Learn,* Peter Gray examines the impact of the lack of play on our youth. Gray suggests that there is a direct relationship between the decline of free play (choice of activities) and the rise of depression. Freedom to play and explore inspire children to learn to solve their own problems, control their own lives, and become competent in pursuing their own interests.

Historians of play contend that the high plateau in children's free play in North America encompassed the first half of the twentieth century. In his book on the history of play in America, Howard Chudacoff refers to this period as "the golden age of unstructured play." By unstructured play, Chudacoff means play that is structured by children themselves rather than by adults, so his term corresponds to what I call free play.

Over the past half century or so, in the United States and in other developed nations, opportunities for children to play, especially to play outdoors with other children, have continually declined. Over this same period, measures of psychopathology in children and adolescents—including indices of anxiety, depression, feelings of helplessness, and narcissism—have continually increased. Research shows a causal link between the decline in play and the increase in psychopathology.

Humans are extraordinarily adaptive to changes in their living conditions, but not infinitely so. I argue that without play, young people fail to acquire the social and emotional skills necessary for healthy psychological development.

Play is needed for healthy brain development

Childhood play stimulates the brain to make connections between nerve cells. These connections help a child develop both gross motor skills (walking, running, jumping, coordination) and fine motor skills (writing, manipulating small tools, detailed hand work).

Play develops the brain's executive function, the mental skills that allow us to manage time and attention, to plan and organize, to remember details, and to decide what is and isn't appropriate to say and do in a given situation. Executive function also helps children learn to master their emotions and to use past experiences to understand how to act in the present. These are the skills that are central to self-control and self-discipline. Kids who have a well-developed executive function do well in school, get along well with others, and make good decisions. Make believe play gives the frontal lobe of the brain, the center of executive function, a workout.

Play with your kids.

Play helps connect family members.

Katie, at 12

Even animals are curious and playful.

Grandparents to the Rescue!

Play strengthens social connections. Laughter is a human response to a social connection. Our emotional systems are designed to share feelings expressed either verbally or through facial expressions and body language.

Grandparents can provide opportunities for play-based interactions that will:

- Increase the neuro pathways connected with learning.
- Enhance memory and organizational abilities.
- Expand problem solving skills.
- Improve well-being.

The current research on play, laughter, fun, and exercise is truly exciting as it indicates promising new ways to treat depression and provide a healthy lifestyle.

The Cat in the Hat is always ready to play! Here he entertains me and Christine.

Toy animals like to dance, too!

Play Triggers Laughter

How do I know that my grandchildren will learn from the laughter? My lifelong journey as detailed in the preface, has taken several unexpected detours. Each step has contributed to my strong belief that grandparents can make a significant difference in the lives of their grandchildren.

Playfulness and laughter will create memories. From the study of cognitive research, we know:

- All learning goes through our emotional filter.
- Play is critical to optimal brain development.
- Play triggers laughter.
- Laughter builds trust and fosters positive communication.

You are never too old. Take time to play.

Teach Kids to See the Funny

Katie and I shared many conversations about the ability to "see the funny" and to choose laughter when things get tough. One time when she was upset about something, I shared with her that when I was young, I would take a pillow when I was angry and furiously beat on it. She laughed in disbelief.

Shortly after her birthday, she sent me a poem that I treasure, and that is a reminder for me to choose "sunshine" when I am feeling frustrated.

A Birthday Poem
By Katie, at 11

I have chosen sunshine.
Not the dark, aged gray.
I have chosen sunshine.
The light that's in today.
I have chosen sunshine.
The brightness in my while.
I have chosen sunshine.
The laughter that makes me smile.
Not rain.
No gloom.
No dust.
No broom.
Trash sadness.
Come here.
No amount of love is out of line.
So that is why I have chosen sunshine.

Katie chooses sunshine wherever she is and whatever she's doing.

We Like Surprises!

"Where are we going, Grandma?"

"It's a surpise."

"Why do you always have surprises for us, Grandma?"
Why indeed...

It is simply because I want to trigger joyful play in your life.

It is because I want you to have memories that will last your entire life—
memories that bring you delight and that tickle your sense of humor over and over again.

I want laughter to be my legacy to you, my miraculous grandchild.

Grandmas Like Surprises, Too!

One day I noticed my grandchildren were giggling behind closed doors. When I went to investigate, I was told by that I was not allowed to enter the room; they were working on a secret project. Hours after they left, I was delighted to find numerous laughter notes scattered throughout the house. They had indeed created surprises for this grandma who for years had been purposefully sharing surprises with them.

BEST Grandma Even

Love, Christine

Grandma Mimi

from katie

I ♥ you from Faith

I love you!!!!

LOVE

1:30

BaseBall/Softball game

captions:
Emma/Ben

Please come and help us win

Free Parents can watch

And then I found this:

A Poem for Grandma

In Dark Times,
You are a Shooting Star.

When we're down you're
a sunbeam of light.

When we aren't having fun,
you make sure we are laughing.

Created by cousins:
Christine and Mimi, both 12

Remember Thing One and Thing Two?

Here is a quick refresher of how information is stored in the long term memory.

THING ONE: Emotions play a critical role in memory.

I invite you to try this experiment. Think back to your earliest memory of elementary school. What is the first thing that you remember? The very first thing…

When recalling that first memory, focus on your feelings. Did the memory stimulate a strong emotion? Vivid memories are most often linked to strong emotions. In second grade, I was put in the coat closet for talking too much. I was really upset, as I did not think it was my fault and it was smelly, dark, and scary. That strong emotional reaction imprinted this experience into my long-term memory. Unfortunately, I do not remember much else from second grade.

During my presentations on humor and play, I invite the audience to participate in this same experiment by recalling school memories. This exercise is a powerful way to illustrate how strong emotions trigger lifelong memories. For some participants, those childhood memories are joyful and pleasant, however, many stories are heartbreaking recollections of embarrassment, shame, fear, and anger. Forty and fifty years after an event, participants will share emotional childhood incidents that have been stored in their hearts and minds. Some of these stories continue to have significant impact on their lives.

Powerful, negative emotional experiences can cause trauma and seriously impact a child's ability to learn. The positive loving support that comes from at least one close relationship is vital for the optimal development of a child. Grandparents are often those unsung superheroes who provide that invaluable emotional support. They can also provide purposeful opportunities for playful engagement in activities that will trigger the laughter needed to reduce anxiety and stress.

Find the Laughter!

A little girl had just finished her first week of school. "I'm just wasting my time," she said to her mother. "I can't read, I can't write, and they won't let me talk!"

Kids will remember how you made them feel. With Ben, age 6.

120

Why Play?

The research is clear—play is essential for cognitive, social, and emotional growth. There is a direct link between the length of play time for an animal species and the comparative level of intelligence. Humans play longer than any other mammal. Children usually play and laugh without much effort if given the space and time to do so. Yet, in our educational systems, there seems to be a widespread effort to suppress spontaneous play in favor of screen-time. Putting electronic devices in the hands of young children is a waste of time compared to the rich learning that occurs during play.

All brains benefit significantly from play. Play is the best tool for maximizing learning and it will significantly enhance the brain development of your grandchild. Here is an example of the research, just in case research is necessary for persuading reluctant family members that the benefits of play supersede electronic devices.

Isaiah, at 6

In studies of juvenile rats, researchers found that play strengthens the social connections between young rodents by producing signals, which are similar to human laughter (Panksepp, 2003). Playing contributes to how young mammals build a memory base in the brain. In mammals, vocalization sounds emerge from tickling and roughhousing activity. In humans, this vocalization is called laughter. Laughter is a human response to a social connection (Provine, 2000).

I cannot emphasize enough that play-filled interactions will profoundly impact your grandchild's life and yours. This loving, interactive relationship can be a delightful alternative to time on devices. If there is an opportunity to begin playful bonding at a young age, kids will be eager for additional grandparent time. It is especially important to offer options that include physical activities that are essential for brain development.

Play is the best tool for maximizing learning.

Relationships Are Built on Interaction

As the child gets older, there are unique opportunities to distract them from their electronic devices by sharing alternative options for fun.

Shared laughter builds trust and lifelong cherished bonds.

Specific skills and knowledge are supported by offering a variety of choices and activities (free-range play.) By engaging in playful experiences, grandparents create a lifetime of memories while supporting optimal brain growth.

See the *Playbook* at the end of this chapter for many ideas for play!

Laugh

be silly

play

Katie drew me a picture of my favorite character—Tigger

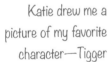

bounce

You can quote me when I say that you are an inspiration to grandmas trying to keep up with modern technology today, and finding ways to bring joy into the lives of her grandchildren through the misuse of slang and hilarious memes.

Katie, at 14

123

Television and video games often have scary images. Art and music offer creative ways to capture those feelings.

Monster robot by Isaiah age 7

Device Advice

How can grandparents nurture these "digital natives" and provide support for the parents in an automated world?

Beginning with the newborn grandchild and throughout their lives, families can engage in playful experiences. This book has countless ideas and playful activities that will maximize brain growth as well as contribute to a loving, close relationship.

Families begin the process of bonding with newborns and building life-long relationships. There is fascinating research on the impact of mirror neurons on our ability to socialize and learn. At all stages we mirror the expressions and actions of those we are in relationship with. The universal practice of parents actively eliciting smiles and laughter is a great example of mirror neurons at work (or at play!). When Isaiah was our newest grandchild, his siblings and cousins smothered him with kisses, hugs, and laughter. At 4 weeks old, he was smiling and responding to their repeated attempts to get him to smile. If you use these same smiling techniques in your everyday life, smiling at strangers, laughing with your family, you will discover these mirror neurons at work.

Of course, the opposite is true. Negativity and frowns also stimulate the mirror neurons. Purposeful use of smiling and laughter can stimulate the positive energy that is possible through mirror neuron activation.

Building trust starts at birth. Top: Katie and her mom enjoy meeting the newest family member, cousin Isaiah.

Left: Christine is thrilled with her new brother, Isaiah. She will soon have him laughing with her.

HELPFUL TIPS

▶ Engage with the child. Watch the show or game with them to help them understand what they're seeing. Comment on things you notice, ask questions about what is happening.

▶ Choose media wisely. Look for age-appropriate apps, games, and programs.

▶ Keep bedtime, mealtime, and family time screen-free. Balancing online and offline time is extremely important.

▶ Limit your own phone use. At a young age, kids model whatever behavior they are seeing.

▶ Emphasize the big three: sleep, healthy nutrition, and exercise. All three are essential to optimal brain growth and development and health and wellness for children and adults alike. And excessive screen time can impact all three.

Jennifer F. Cross, M.D.
Pediatric Behavior & Development

Technology and Play

Technology continues to advance at a rapid pace providing new innovations that continuously impact the way we live. There are great interactive options that engage technology for large muscle activities or to inspire the creativity in your grandchild. Many of us depend on our grandchildren's knowledge to guide us through the increasingly complicated world of everchanging technologies.

Thank goodness they are tech savvy and can help us with technology survival skills!

Christine, Katie, and Samuel play virtual soccer at Discovery Center Museum in Rockford, Illinois.

I was grateful to Ben for his technology skills while trying to connect our Alaska trip pictures from the computer to the television screen.

Don, husband

Tyler tries an airplane simulator at Discovery Center Museum.

Then and Now

Ben's interest in technology and computers has resulted in his completing a college curriculum in technology and a job in the field.

126

I've always been fascinated with flying things. My love for aerospace began years ago when I was just starting my first 4-H project in model rocketry. The feeling it gave me to be able to create a rocket and watch it fly to incredible heights helped me to see that I can do whatever I set my mind to.

Samuel, 17, plans to become an aeronautical engineer

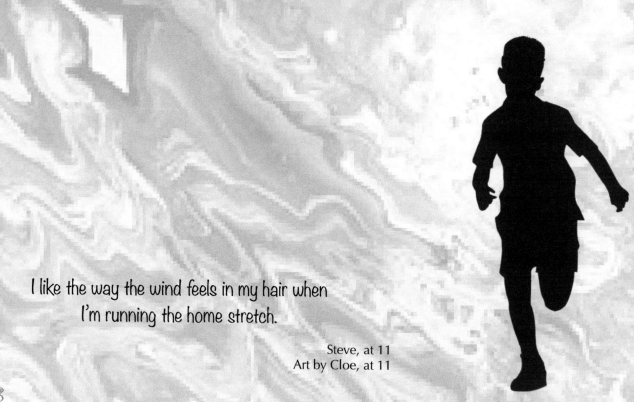

I like the way the wind feels in my hair when
I'm running the home stretch.

Steve, at 11
Art by Cloe, at 11

To be contued.

Art by Faith, at 6

129

Play leads to brain plasticity,
adaptability and creativity.
Nothing fires up the brain
like play.

–Stuart Brown

THE GRAND

Playbook

Legacy of Laughter

A Playbook for the Stages of Humor Development

This playbook is designed to share some ideas that we have found successful. Sharing playful activities with your grandchild will not only nurture them, but it will energize you.

This chapter aligns the 5 basic stages of humor development (Morrison, 2008) with a PLAYBOOK GUIDE. While numerous examples of play are woven throughout this book, the recommendations in this chapter are age specific. Of course, your grandchild is quite gifted, so you may want to read ahead to the next stage!

Grandparents have a hidden superpower. They develop a special relationship with their grandchild that includes active, playful fun.

Peek-a-Boo
Birth to Two Years

There is a universal pattern to the initial stage of humor development beginning with an infant learning to laugh. The simple game of Peek-a-Boo illustrates the three-part structure. Anxiety followed by surprise leads to relieved laughter.

1. Mild Anxiety: Caregiver's face is hidden for a very short time (often with a blanket).

2. Surprise: The blanket is taken away to see smiling caregiver.

3. Relief: The child is reassured to see caregiver and there is shared laughter.

When this pattern is frequently repeated, the baby learns to anticipate and participate in laughter. This basic, timeless laughter process is initiated across cultures and is a vital characteristic of human development.

The peek-a-boo interaction with your baby provides a foundation for many subsequent playful activities including the age-old game of Hide and Seek. Surprise will continue to evoke a laughter response throughout life. Many comedy routines are set up using this format to incorporate the element of surprise including ageless television shows such as *Candid Camera* and *America's Funniest Home Videos*.

Parents attempt all sorts of crazy antics to elicit that first smile from their newborn. Look back at the early pictures of your own children. Yep—baby books feature those first smiles. There is a reason that the most popular social media videos feature laughing babies. Laughter is contagious and watching that video provides instant stress relief.

The Peek-a-Boo stage builds the foundation of trust and hope that is necessary for emotional intelligence and for building relationships.

1

Literacy

▶ Rock and Read, Read, Read: This is absolutely one of the best ways to nurture brain development. *And, it is great for the baby, too!*

▶ Engage in conversations: Share your favorite childhood memories. Whisper your deep secrets. They will be absorbing language and understand much more than you realize. Bilingual skills are a bonus opportunity for increasing cognitive growth.

▶ Baby Sign Language: This use of gestures allows infants and toddlers to communicate emotions, desires and needs prior to spoken language. To learn about basic infant sign language, you can find information online.

Games

▶ Generate bubbles at bath time by adding a bit of shampoo to the water.

▶ Manipulate puppets to engage in playful, silly conversations.

▶ Fill a small plastic bowl with water and put on top of the highchair. Add some mismatched Tupperware pieces, a funnel and/or a plastic strainer. Keep a towel handy.

▶ Enjoy creative baby toys. The Bumble Ball was our favorite—it generated much adult laughter while it kept Ben and Tyler quite entertained when they started to crawl.

Music/Drama

▶ Sing lullabies while rocking to sleep. They will not notice if you are off key!

▶ Engage in the magic of fingerplays. These short repetitive rhyming phrases include hand movements and will spark your baby's interest. "Where is Thumbkin?" was a favorite.

▶ Music maximizes brain development. Let them experiment with different instruments.

▶ Mix the words up in familiar songs. When singing *Old McDonald Had a Farm*, change the "quack, quack" to "meow, meow." This silly adaptation always elicited squeals of laughter from Mimi and shouts of "NOOOO Grandma! Ducks go quack!

I have no idea how many children's books I've enjoyed with the grandkids over the last 20 years. Often, the adventures in the stories were so exhausting, we took a nap together in the recliner to recover.

Don Morrison, extraordinary husband of author

Arts and Crafts

▶ Scribbling with crayons can begin at 15 months. Be sure to save a few of these initial works of art with the date.

Outdoors, Science, and Nature

▶ Observe birds and chat about their songs, color, and species.

▶ Discover butterflies and gently touch caterpillars.

▶ Delight in their first experience of feeling grass and touching flowers.

Food Stuff

▶ Put various small pieces of edible foods on their high-chair tray as you are cooking. Talk about the color and texture. Their expressions are priceless photo opportunities.

▶ Finger-painting with pudding seemed like a relatively easy clean-up until I found several chocolate globs in their hair a bath time.

Grasshoppers by Steven, at 12

Knock-Knock
Two Years to School Age

Dragon by Katie, at 14

Pretending, exaggeration, and creativity emerge in this stage of humor development. The world of fantasy emerges during the stage of development. Your grandkids will become engrossed in make-believe activities with their imagination reflected in silly stories and fantasy drawings. Their dramatic play usually imitates adult activities.

Taboo words and laughter about body parts are common in early childhood. Jokes about elimination and "private" body parts are often accompanied with giggles.

At age two-and-a-half Samuel declared that his grandma was sure silly when she sang and exaggerated the movements to several songs. Of course, Samuel was right, as I frequently embellish silly behavior to elicit laughter.

Imagine *Create*

Kids this age start to engage in conversations.

Make Music

137

Literacy

▶ Read silly rhyme books: Dr. Seuss books are a favorite.

▶ Share knock-knock jokes as a way for them to learn comedy patterns.

▶ Expand their vocabulary by reading and playing word games.

▶ Plan field trips to museums, conservatories, and parks.

Use scribble pictures or their artwork to send as thank you notes. Help them write their names on these.

Jan Jakeway, friend

Games/Activities

▶ Experiment with a variety of games. Each grandchild had their preferences. While you may want to purchase a few favorites, you can borrow some from your local library to experiment with varied games.

▶ Create a sensory box. Cut hand-sized holes in the top of a shoebox. Put various items inside to touch without being able to see them. Ask if they can guess what is in the box. Try various items: cotton, squishy ball, crayon, spinner, or even an ice cube—anything that would be stimulating to touch.

▶ Create a fort or cave (a large blanket over a small table works well).

▶ Design a playhouse: Cut a door and window into the sides of a huge box. Appliance boxes really are the best. Decorate with crayons or paint.

▶ Create flashlight creatures in a dark room. Start a spooky story and have your grandchild finish the tale.

▶ Suggest a theme: grocery store, doctor office, restaurant. Provide simple props.

Music/Dance/Drama

▶ Sing silly songs. Add outrageous actions. Old camp songs are usually my first choice.

▶ Rock to the chicken dance or the Hokey Pokey

▶ Attempt Karaoke. Yes—You can!

▶ Play an instrument you learned as a child (dust off that ukulele).

▶ Use songs to encourage picking up toys, washing hands or brushing teeth.

Arts and Crafts

▶ Make collages by cutting pictures from old magazines. Glue these onto a piece of paper or onto a cut-out brown paper bag. Monitor emerging scissor skills (these small muscle skills develop around the age of 4). Glue sticks are a preferred choice for this age.

▶ Footprint pictures: Paint their feet with acrylic paint, have them step on sturdy paper. Keep a tub of warm water and towels handy. An easier version is to trace around hands for a different creative art experience.

▶ Fashion paper hats, paper airplanes or origami.

Outdoors, Science, and Nature

▶ Plant a vegetable garden. Put a few small seeds in a container or small dish so they are do not all spill in one garden spot! That combination of water and dirt may be messy but will rapidly accelerate learning.

▶ Simply let them run around outside and scream in delight! Join them.

▶ Arrange for some water play. Fill a large container with water, add some plastic containers, funnels and strainers and let them splash away. Add bubbles for additional wonder.

▶ Take wagon and bike rides. A trip to the neighborhood park can become an unexpected adventure. Ask why is that dog barking and how did that paper end up in the ditch?

▶ Pick flowers. Put individual flowers in between waxed paper and press in a large book. Add some weight on top. When dry, these can be glued in a collage on black paper. Dandelions are always a treasured gift from children. Put them in a vase with water.

▶ Capture caterpillars or insects and create a "hotel" for these little creatures. Let the kids know that the hotel is only good for a short visit. Talk about the importance of a release so they can go back to their own homes. It can be traumatic for young children to find a dead bug in the jar.

Ben and Tyler really enjoy blowing bubbles outside.

Music maximizes brain development. Let them experiment with different instruments.

Stone Soup

Cooking with Grandparents

▶ Make a pot of Stone Soup. Start with a stone* and proceed using the various ingredients mentioned in the book. Add vegetable broth or bouillon cubes.

Note: Bleach a smooth stone and boil it in a separate pot before using it in the soup.

▶ Carve a pumpkin, scoop out the seeds and toast. Toss with a bit of butter and salt. Bake for 40 minutes at 300 degrees.

▶ Discover the star in an apple. Cut an apple horizontally to see the "star." There are several wonderful children's books that can supplement this activity. Dip the slices in peanut butter for a nutritious snack.

▶ Peel a potato or carrot. Start by demonstrating how to push the peeler away from the body.

▶ Follow a recipe that they have chosen. Encourage them to read some of the words. Making tapioca with Cloe involved discussing the difference between tablespoons and teaspoons.

▶ Wash dishes. Pull a stool up to the sink so they can enjoy washing the plastic dishes over and over again. "This is my favorite thing to do" Faith, age 6.

▶ Create edible plate art. Arrange food in different shapes to create animals, flowers or other objects. Pinterest has more ideas than you can try in a lifetime.

EGGS!

A super skill to learn at Grandma's house:

Learning to CRACK an egg.

Teach them to crack an egg (as early as 16 months). They will take huge delight in seeing what is inside the egg. Keep a wet cloth available to wipe their hands.

Steve was always happy when he was successfully able to crack the egg into a bowl without any shells. "My kids loved baking with you: breaking eggs was a BIG DEAL when they were little."

Julie, daughter-in-law- Steve's mom

Smoochie Moochie

Isha is a puppet
who lives in cherry juice.

He puts his ears onto his eyes
when he is in the juice.

He can see with his ears.

He has an eyeball in his mouth.

Isaiah, at 6

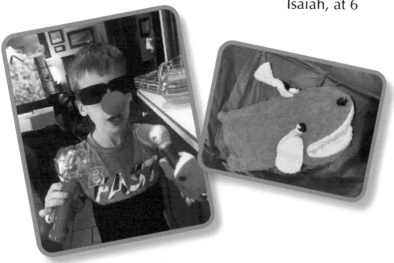

Create a story using puppets. Sock puppets can
be easily created from that collection of mismatched socks. This is one of my favorite stories
that was created when Isaiah discovered an old
well-worn pink puppet at our house.

Riddle-De-Dee

Early Primary Years

You are a superhero to your grandchild. Use your super powers to
persuade some device downtime. A powerful persuasion activity is
reading together, sharing stories, and repeating those activities that
you enjoy together.

Food preparation is usually a huge hit. Tempt your grandchild with
nature exploration, art and music, and vigorous physical activity.

Grandparents can have a significant role in modeling humor
and interjecting laughter into difficult situations. There are many
strategies you can use to initiate fun into conversations with your
grandchildren.

Practice riddles, laugh at their silly antics, and read funny books. A
grasp of irony seems to emerge about six years of age and riddles and
jokes will be appreciated.

What did the ocean say
to the beach??
NOTHING! It just waved.

Laugh Outloud

"What did the little corn say to the mama corn?"

Where is POP corn?

3

"What is a tree's favorite drink?"

Root beer!

Literacy

▶ Introduce joke and riddles! Even reluctant readers will be tempted to try reading joke, riddle and comic books. Let them practice the joke and riddles on you.

▶ Post some riddles on the refrigerator door. Invite them to figure out the answer. Before they come, put a variety of riddles on index cards and see if they can solve them. Let them take these home to try on their parents.

▶ Find creative ways to help with homework: Learn spelling words by drawing the letters on the ceiling with a flashlight.

▶ Attend funny movies. There are many great children's movies that have subtle underlying humor specifically intended for the adults watching the film. Afterwards ask them about the funniest part of the movie. Invite them to write a movie review.

Games/Activities

▶ Board and card games are a MUST at this age. Our favorites include: Apples to Apples, Blank Slate, and Tapple.

▶ Plan ahead for activities when traveling in the car. Wrap presents for each child to open when boredom sets in. Create travel BINGO sheets or do the alphabet game where starting with finding something that starts with the letter "A" and continuing through "Z." Can also look for the actual letter if it is impossible to find the letter "X" for example.

▶ We always have snacks during family games—popcorn is a favorite.

▶ Day Trip Adventures: Plan ahead!

▶ Library: Not only a great place to find books, but an invaluable resource for programs and activities.

▶ County Fairs: Review the schedule of events and consider attendance during the kid's day programs.

▶ Museum events: Search for special events and upcoming exhibits. Grandparent passes are often available.

This is a favorite memory with Cloe! Say yes to amusement park rides—unless they want to do the death defying roller coaster!

▶ A zoo trip is always captivating. Check out the feeding schedules online before you go.

▶ Plan ahead for activities when traveling by car. Wrap presents for each child to open when boredom sets in. I often create travel BINGO sheets. Or play the alphabet game; start with finding something that begins with the letter "A" and continue through "Z." Look for the actual letter if it is impossible to find the letter (for example X or Q).

Music/Drama

▶ Form a Grandma's Marching Band: Play lively parade music. Supply a variety of home-made instruments and encourage them to march. This is a great activity for cousins.

▶ Get sing-along books for the car.

▶ Find a family theme song (for our 12 grands—it was the 12 days of Christmas). Enact the song or create dance routines.

▶ Dance parties: Just put on some dance music and exhibit your best moves. They will join in or roll their eyes and laugh! Share the dance moves you learned in high school and they will laugh again.

▶ Invite your grandchild to play their instrument. Andrew often entertained us with his guitar and Emma with her flute.

Arts and Crafts

▶ Finger paint by spraying shaving cream on a baking sheet. This activity is an easy clean-up! Use old t-shirts to protect clothes.

▶ Design a fairy garden. Visit a greenhouse for ideas and supplies. Our local venue donated some clean dirt for the base and pebbles for the paths. A large boot or shoebox works well for a first attempt. Fill with sand or dirt and watch their imaginations flourish. Faith loved creating her special garden and rearranges the fairy figures over and over again.

▶ Play-Doh®: I usually buy this at the dollar store but there are recipes online to create your own. Provide a variety of measuring cups and small plates. Use a marker to create "burners" on top of an empty shoe box so they can "cook" you a meal. Emma always enjoyed making food for us to taste. Of course, we took great delight in letting her know that it was delicious . . . or that it needed more salt.

Faith's Fairy Garden

Outdoors, Science and Nature

▶ Go on a toad hunt. Use a net and bring a container. Look for these elusive creatures under rocks and in swampy areas.

▶ Katie caught a toad for Cloe at our house. Toadie now lives in an amphibian house in her bedroom. There have been several toads caught in our yard and so I just saved the container for any captured creatures.

▶ Climb
  • Climbing trees are so much fun.
  • Rock climbing is also a great adventure.
  • Faith testing her balance when she climbed up on the stone wall.

▶ Capture lightening bugs (fireflies). Demetra and Jaime, our nieces from California, had never experienced these delightful creatures and were enchanted to see them light up in a glass jar.

▶ Look for and identify birds. See if you can find a nest or a feather. Try to guess what kind of bird it belonged to. Bird books help to identify the birds at the feeder.

▶ Science experiments can be fun. Experiment with making volcanoes, shoot rockets, or explore what happens with air currents from ceiling fans.

We use the fire pit often. Mary Kay gathers the supplies for S'mores, and I get the fire ready for roasting marshmallows. The cold fire pit also was a haven for toads and the kids like to dig through the coals to find them.

Don Morrison

146

Cooking with Grandparents

▶ Read the book *Stone Soup* (again). I know I am repeating this activity—it has been one of the most requested activities from our grandchildren.

▶ Try blindfold taste tests. Buy several varieties of apples and discuss which is the tartest or sweetest. See if they can guess the flavor of green grape versus the purple grape. Taste test different flavors of yogurt.

▶ Create Monster Pancakes. This was the number one favorite breakfast every morning of overnight stays at our house.

Another thing we did was monster pancakes. Now these were of course, pancakes, with a twist. Chocolate chips, craisins and nuts arranged into a face with syrup and on top. Delicious, messy and fun. These were perfect and a great part of my childhood.

Favorite memory from Ben

Isaiah's Muffin Maker Story

I woke up at 5:25 a.m. I went downstairs, and Grandma warmed up the oven while we sat and talked with the lions. (Grandma note—yep, these are stuffed animals). I put the cupcake liners in the pan. And I helped Grandma put the dough in the liners. I put the drizzle of brown sugar and butter on the muffins. Then Grandma put the muffins in the oven. Grandpa came in the kitchen and he said, "Yum, yum, yum." Isaiah at 6

147

Pun Fun

Long fairy tales have a tendency to dragon.

Gift them with books written specifically for teens. My favorite is: "Find Your Funny: The Humor Survival Guide" by Barb Best & Joanne Jackal.

Children at this stage are moving toward an increased understanding of the subtle differences in language. Word play, language variations, and the magic of the English language become a magnet that can captivate children from age 10 through teen years.

Observe when your grandchild can first detect and enjoy a language twist in stories. Notice when they are able to "get the joke." Puns and gentle satire are appreciated at this age. They may begin to make up their own jokes and they will laugh hysterically at their own genius.

Do not be afraid to try crazy, out-of-the box activities. Keeping plans a secret until the day of the activity adds to the suspense and fun. Kids love to guess what you have planned for surprises on their special day.

The middle years initiate the emergence of puberty, with jokes about sex and the emergence of hormonal behavior. Adolescents experience anxiety about physical changes they experience, and sexual humor can provide relief from the stress of puberty. Physical changes evoke challenges for preteens, who resort to laughing with others as a coping device. Unfortunately, it is often a stage where peers might laugh at them, not with them. Many teens experience or participate in bullying behavior.

Playful teasing can be fun when there is mutual trust. Discuss the difference between playful teasing and bullying. "If the impact is hurtful, it is inappropriate, even if the intent is not harmful" (Morrison, 2008). At this age they start to create jokes to let you know that they are kidding.

148

The best April Fool jokes are the ones that keep on giving. One year, I went to my daughter's house when the family was gone and attached googly eyes to everything in the cupboard and refrigerator. When they pulled out the milk carton or cereal box, they found silly eyes staring at them. Googly eyes can be put on virtually anything—toothpaste tubes, lampshades, and laundry detergent, even a love note slipped into a pocket!

Kathy Laurenhue, friend, from Wiser Now newsletter

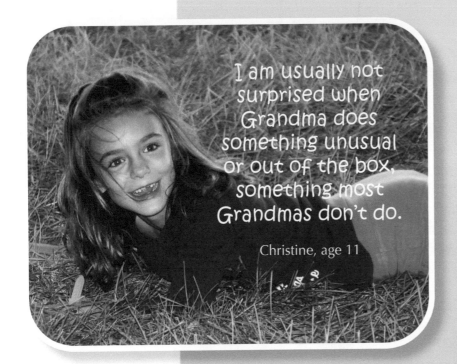

I am usually not surprised when Grandma does something unusual or out of the box, something most Grandmas don't do.

Christine, age 11

Geology rocks but Geography is where it's

Explore the element of surprise.

Literacy

▶ Joke books are a must! Cartoons and memes are fun to send via text.

▶ Create vision boards to assist with memory work. Using old magazines, cut out pictures related to the subject to be learned. Glue the pictures onto a poster board or into a study assistance notebook. Invite them to create a riddle or joke about the lesson.

Games

▶ In-house Hide and Seek—a favorite is "Sardines" where one person hides, and everyone tries to find them. When found, they hide with them until the last person finds the group. This has been a favorite game for Samuel. Be prepared to find clothes on the floor in your closets. One year, Steve hid under the Christmas tree.

▶ Charades are fun with grandchildren groups especially when they create the challenge words.

▶ Lego kits or puzzles are quieter activities that can be fun with grandparents.

▶ Board games are great fun for the entire family. Some of our favorites: Blurt, Monopoly, Yahtzee, Pictionary, Mega Mouth.

Blurt!

The part of a plane or spacecraft where the pilot sits
COCKPIT!

An archer's case for holding arrows
QUIVER!

A machine that cuts documents into pieces so that no one can read them
SHREDDER!

Blurt!

1 or 2 The nut of an oak tree
ACORN!

3 or 4 A place where coins are made
MINT!

5 or 6 A young dog
PUPPY!

Music/Drama

▶ Host a cousin movie night at your house. Have a popcorn bar with nuts and various toppings.

▶ Several of the pre-teens have asked to play their favorite radio station when we are driving. Commercials are a great time to discuss the lyrics and learn more about current teen music and culture.

▶ Invite children to write a basic screenplay and enact it.

▶ Concerts, plays, and movies are great options. Emma was excited for a trip to the Fireside Theater for a dinner theater event with her mom and grandparents.

The games Blurt, Mega Mouth (pictured above), and Tribond were created by my friend Tim Walsh, co-founder of Roo Games.

The best part about jazz band is when you have anxiety that your solo won't go well but then it sounds amazing.

Steve, at 13

Arts and Crafts

▶ Enroll in an art class together. Christine and I enjoyed taking an oil class together at Nicholas Conservatory.

▶ Paint with acrylics on a variety of materials. This is a good age to experiment with painting on canvas or wood. Steve painted an amazing rooster for me to add to the large collection of roosters in my house. Rock monsters can be painted, sprayed with lacquer, and placed in an outdoor garden.

▶ Try block-print art using cut potatoes, leaves, or even fish.

▶ Experiment with different art materials. A package of pipe cleaners can offer endless opportunities. Oil pastels and clay are great mediums to introduce at this age.

Outdoors, Science, and Nature

▶ Stargazing: There are intriguing apps that can help identify the night sky. Lie on a blanket on the ground and use a flashlight to point out the stars. Be sure to share the story of the milky-way and other constellations.

▶ Forest preserves and conservation districts offer endless opportunities for nature walks, exhibits and programs.

▶ Spontaneous play is such fun. It is especially exciting when there is an announcement that school is closed for the day. A snow day can provide unanticipated fun time spent in the outdoors!

Foodstuff

▶ Request that they make a dish for the family gathering. Christine made a delicious Baked Alaska for one of our Christmas parties. It was fun for all of us to watch her start it on fire.

▶ Invite your grandchild to make and submit recipes for a family cookbook that includes their favorite food ideas. When we made homemade macaroni and cheese together, Tyler added a secret ingredient to this recipe. It is a now a family favorite.

▶ Host a fancy meal. Plan the menu and prep the food together. Set the table, create a centerpiece, and take out the fancy dishes. Invite the grandkids to help clean up after the meal. Play lively music, sing or dance while doing the dishes.

▶ At a family gathering ask for assistance with taking dessert orders from the adults. Children are delighted when they can add add sky-high mounds of ice cream or whipped cream.

Cloe spent hours creating collages including this girl on a swing which hangs from the ceiling in her room.

5

Maximizes Joyful Living

Joy Flow

Maturing Humor Style—
High School to Adult

The ultimate goal for maturation of a humor being is for optimal growth and self-discovery. A humor being views life's challenges with optimistic amusement. A heightened state of positive emotionality is the goal of this stage.

When adults are having fun and laughing, theu provide a positive model for grandchildren. Playing with your older grandchild will add life to your years. Becoming aware of one's own sense of humor provides an opportunity to expand humergy through humor practice. This experience of laughter's flow and the emerging energy will create a natural euphoric high that will be a model for your grandchild.

As your grandchild becomes a young adult, continue to engage in playful interactions and shared laughter. Let them know that you appreciate the laughter they bring to your life.

Literacy

▶ Encourage your grandchildren to write about their memories with you. Create a book with these memories. Notice what happened to me with this process! You might just write a book like I did!

▶ Read funny obituaries together. Notice how frequently humor is mentioned as an admired attribute when memorializing a life. Humor and laughter are indeed a legacy that is frequently shared at memorials. Read an obituary about someone you knew, share it with your grandchild along with your favorite memories. This is an opportune time to initiate a conversation about grief. You may be one of the few people who will have this kind of opportunity to discuss this difficult topic. Remind them that laughter is what people often remember about the loved one who has died.

Emotional intelligence is a factor in appreciating and learning to use humor.

Games

▶ Along with previous suggestions- here are some others that our teenagers enjoy.

▶ Scavenger Hunt: Emma designed her own version of a scavenger hunt when we were on our 8th grade trip and had to wait in the small airport. She walked around with her grandpa, finding unique items or signs. She made a creative list of things for me to find. It was a great activity to keep us entertained in what could have been a long wait time in a boring airport.

▶ Board and Cards are a great way to connect with teens. Favorites include: Pit, Scrabble, Telestrations, 5 Crowns, Spoons, and 7-Up (card game).

Music/Damce/Drama

▶ Dance together with a music video that illustrates the moves.

▶ Attend a live dinner theater production.

> When I went to Grandma's house, we had a tradition of playing card games, the most popular is 7-Up. While I wasn't terrible at it, I had fallen into a trend where I would lose no matter what. After about three years, I finally broke that losing streak. NO matter what I always ended up having fun.
>
> **Tyler, at 17**

Arts and Crafts

► Make hand crafted greeting cards.

► Do silhouette self-portraits. Tape paper to the wall. Use a flashlight to outline the face on black paper. Cut and paste on white background.

► Plan a trip to an art museum and request any education materials to optimize the learning. The Chicago Art Museum has educational materials and programs for students. Samuel really enjoyed finding works of art on the recommended list.

Outdoors, Science, and Nature

► Sprinklers and water projectiles: teenagers especially enjoy dousing each other with an unexpected water spraying.

► Water balloon toss contests can be quite animated. Be prepared to get wet.

► Initiate flashlight adventures at night. Hide and Seek and/or scavenger hunts in the dark can be thrilling. An open field is the perfect place for flashlight tag.

► Fire pit activities include camp songs, cooking kabobs, or roasting marshmallows for s'mores.

► Tree climbing, hiking, and ziplining can be an awesome challenge, especially for the grandparent. Emma requested that we go zip-lining for her 8th grade trip. It was scary for all of us, but a ton of fun.

► Indoor rock climbing walls and trampoline parks are perfect for tweens and teens, especially in bad weather.

► Rent paddle boats or canoes. Insist that they wear safety vests.

► Fly kites. Blow bubbles. Toss bean bags. Throw balls.

► Catch worms at night for fishing the next day. Turn the hose on for an hour and the worms will come close to the surface.

► National Parks are amazing places to hike. We saw a black bear near the trail on Emma's 8th grade trip.

Foodstuff

► Plan a "Create Your Own ___" party. Provide basic ingredients and a variety of toppings for everyone to make their own. Some ideas: Pizza, Taco, Baked Potato, Ice Cream, Popcorn and Candy.

► Grill cheese sandwiches and serve with tomato soup.

► Monster pancakes never get old!

On Becoming a Humor Being

As I continue to study and teach about the neuroscience of humor, I have found that the workshop sessions that I present on "Humor and Aging" are becoming increasingly popular. These sessions begin with participants answering the question:

"At what age do you think you become old?"

The responses vary, but after lively conversation, it is generally agreed that age is a state of mind.

A youthful frame of mind can have a powerful effect on both physical aging and mental abilities. In a groundbreaking experiment, scientists prepared an environment designed to induce a younger subjective age in participants. Various methods were used to backpeddle the mindset. One technique involved creating an atmosphere similar to what participants experienced in their teens and early 20s. After a week of living in an environment with the music, movies and atmosphere of their youth, most of these adults became more capable on both physical and mental tasks.

Humergy

Extraordinary optimism and a passionate energy for life, combined with a gentle understanding of others. This term describes the energy that radiates the optimistic joy of our inner spirit, reflects our unique personality, and nourishes a healthy mind/body balance.

Joy Flow

Joy flow is the degree to which we accomplish optimal growth and self-discovery. This peak experience exemplifies the capacity to view challenges with optimistic amusement. A heightened state of positive emotionality defines this peak experience. For many, joy flow is almost a spiritual journey.

Play and Playfulness

Play and playfulness are critical components for keeping a youthful mindset. Having grandchildren is known to contribute to longevity. I suspect it is because grandparents laugh with their grandchildren.

May you experience boundless humergy and laughter through play and playfulness as you create your own legacy of laughter.

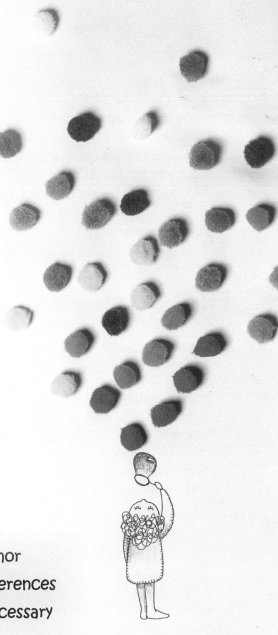

The ability to recognize the variances in language is essential for humor development. Your grandchild is developing the capacity to perceive differences between feelings of joy, surprise, silliness, happiness, and sarcasm—all necessary elements for humor development.

Legacy of Laughter: The Journey

I want to live forever in the hearts of my grandchildren.

How will your grandchildren remember you? The positive loving support that comes from close relationships is vital for the optimal development of a child. Grandparents have an extraordinary opportunity to make a *ginormous* (Isaiah's word) impact on lives of their grandchildren. When purposefully engaging in playful activities with your grandchild, you generate memories that will last a lifetime.

Play tickles the funny bone while nurturing physical strength, mental agility, and social skills. Play is vital not only for the growth and development of a child, but it is enormously beneficial for adults as well. Sharing playful activities with a grandchild will not only nurture them but will energize grandparents as well.

My own experiences with our grandchildren have been created together with my husband Don, who was a middle school teacher and is a lifelong educator. He always jokes that it took him 20 years to get out of middle school. His career path included many roles as an education administrator, which he jokingly describes as going to the "dark" side. Many of the ideas found in this book including the 8th grade trips and the kids' woodland paths were generated with his ingenuity. This book certainly would not have been written without his contributions.

How the Heck Did I End Up Writing this Book?

At a recent networking group, I was asked to share what I do. The response that I teach courses and workshops in humor studies was met with an incredulous: "You teach what?" As I laughed, I had to admit that I am as surprised by this unexpected career as the person who asked the question. As with most people, my life journey has involved many ups and downs! I call them squats! My

passion has been to explore and maximize the benefits of humor and play in my own life and in the lives of others. This focus has emerged from various jobs in the field of education, from my lifelong interest in brain research, and from my curiosity about how humor impacts learning. The most significant insights have emerged from my attempts to find the funny in my own life. There have been times when my sense of humor has been buried under piles and piles of life's stuff. I am grateful to the people along the way who have helped me dig out of the mess to find the laughter.

Grandparents are those unsung superheroes who can quietly but effectively optimize brain development and provide a unique Legacy of Laughter.

And yes, my grandchildren have been most effective in helping me experience the lighter side of life.

It Began with My Job as a Kindergarten Teacher

Armed with a degree in early childhood, and trained in strategies for integrating purposeful play in the curriculum, I eagerly began my career teaching 5-year-olds. My university preparation had cultivated a deep interest into how the seemingly simple act of kids playing profoundly impacts brain development. I became immersed in the philosophy and in the power of play.

But BAM! Reality hit when I was faced with a mandated school curriculum that violated many of my beliefs and challenged my efforts to integrate play into the kindergarten classroom. I persisted in providing a play curriculum in spite of a skeptical administrator. It was a rocky first year. However, my lifelong interest in studying how play impacts learning came out of those early teaching experiences. The distress that I observed in the faces of my kindergarten students during the administration of lengthy paper and pencil tests triggered my passion to learn more about the brain and learning. A firm belief that play, laughter, and humor were critically important to learning were supported by emerging cognitive research. And I realized that in spite of the frustration of the mandates, I absolutely loved watching kids learn through play.

The Powerful Impact of Parenting

After two years of teaching kindergarten, I was delighted to learn that we were expecting our first child. Our four extraordinary children were born close together, within six years. The memories from those years are foggy and interspersed with flashbacks of endless laundry, constant cooking, and the struggle of trying to balance parenting and a career.

While details are vague, I vividly remember the hot tears that flooded my eyes after a parent-teacher conference when I learned that my son was having serious challenges in school. How could a child who was obviously so bright, be unable to sit still? After moving him back and forth between schools, he was finally diagnosed with attention deficit disorder (ADD) in 7th grade. This was before much was known about brain function, and before there was an understanding of the differentiation between ADD, attention-deficit/hyperactivity disorder (ADHD), and other modes of learning.

My son and I were both relieved to learn that the unique composition of his brain contributed to his endless energy, impulsive creativity, and his remarkable and exceptional skills. His learning style was quite different from those of his older brother who experienced some early difficulty with learning to read, but who, by the age of 9 could take apart the engine of a lawn mower and effortlessly put it back together. How could this gifted, young mechanic have difficulties learning to read? My fervent desire to nurture and support my own children, along with my experience as an educator fueled my passion to explore the neuroscience of learning.

Career Opportunities

Degrees in early childhood and educational administration provided a foundation for my interest in play, but it is important to mention a few other experiences that have contributed a unique perspective for writing this book. One significant experience included several years of working in a general educational diploma (GED) and teen parent program at the community college. While providing occupational guidance for adults who had dropped out of school, I heard painful stories about their educational experiences. They shared vivid memories of the shame and guilt they felt about not being able to succeed in school.

Another foundational career opportunity came from my work at a Regional Office of Education, where my role was to provide staff development opportunities for educators. As part of that responsibility, I had the opportunity to attend numerous conferences related to brain science and learning. When I asked my mentor and brain science guru Bob Sylwester what he knew about the brain and humor, he replied that if I could discover that, I would be considered for the Nobel Peace Prize. At that time the research on humor and the brain was somewhat limited.

Humor research continues to be a complex exploration in the field of neuroscience. Over the past 40 years, I have been blessed to interact with people from all walks of life who have contributed and shared ideas about the brain, current research, and humor practice. Serving on the board and as president of the Association for Applied and Therapeutic Humor (AATH) has provided invaluable interactions with professionals from all over the world. As founder and director of the AATH Humor Academy, I have mentored and learned from students who explored the application of humor in their research-based projects. This community of humor enthusiasts continues to share the research and strategies that support humor research and applications in various fields.

My second book, Using Humor to Maximize Living is the textbook for the Humor Academy, as well as for numerous other courses related to humor studies. Many of the ideas in this textbook created the foundation for Legacy of Laughter.

It has been enlightening to work with people worldwide who have been actively integrating humor and play into both their personal and professional lives. Serving on the board and as president of AATH provided invaluable interactions with humor experts from all over the world. My books are used internationally and have been translated into several languages.

Through my work at the Humor Academy, I continue to mentor students in the theory and application of humor research projects.

As much as I appreciated my various career opportunities, my most valued experiences have been in my role as a parent and grandparent. The mix of career and personal experiences has blessed me with a unique perspective on how grandparents can make a significant impact on the lives of their grandchildren. One of the most joyful times of my life has been to collaborate with my grandchildren on this book, *Legacy of Laughter: A Grandparent Guide and Playbook*.

The Grandparent Sauce: A Mix of Family and Friends

As each of the 12 grandchildren were born, I cherished the joy of being together, laughing, and bonding with them. These spontaneous experiences eventually evolved into a conscious awareness. I realized that I was being intentional in creating fun playful experiences while developing a close relationship with each of them.

This journey did not begin with the intent to study the benefits of laughter with my grandchildren. However, when high school friend Kathy Carney Brown paid me a visit and saw the 12 sets of keys on

a key rack and the 12 multicolored totes filled with "office stuff," she insisted that I had an obligation to share my philosophy and ideas with other grandparents. Several other friends also nudged me in the direction of writing a book.

I had previously invited my grandchildren to write about our experiences together in a family journal. These scribbled notes and their insights along with the encouragement of countless others eventually contributed to this book. It has been an unexpected blessing to put into writing what I have learned from countless playful experiences with my grandchildren.

Writing this book has allowed me to flourish in ways that I never dreamed possible. I hope my readers will relish the somewhat scattered, but bountiful, joyful journey that I have been blessed to experience with my grandchildren. They have left an invigorated spirit as well as a lasting imprint on my heart.

It is my hope that by sharing this guide and playbook that you, the reader, will create your own unique Legacy of Laughter.

Author's Note: This book is written with the recognition that the ideas in here just scratch the surface of the range of possibilities. It is recognized that many grandparents face limitations that will impact their ability to implement many of the suggestions in this book. These will include distance, finances, family dynamics, and culture. My hope is that each grandparent will adapt using their own special sauce to create their own legacy of laughter.

For more information, visit:
HUMOR QUEST
www.questforhumor.com

Explore Your Neighborhood

Many of our adventures take place in our home state of Illinois. We appreciate the fabulous opportunities for grandparent experiences made possible by these organizations. Take the time to explore your own neighborhood. You never know what wonders abound!

Rockford, and Surrounding Area

- Anderson Japanese Gardens
- BMO Harris Bank Center
- Boone County Fairgrounds
- Burpee Museum of Natural History
- Coronado Performing Arts Center
- Discovery Center Museum
- Edwards Christmas Tree Farm
- Klehm Arboretum and Botanic Garden
- Midway Village and Museum Center
- Nicholas Conservatory
- Rock Cut State Park
- Rockford Art Museum
- Rockford Park District
- Rockford Sportscore
- Severson Dells Nature Center
- Sinnissippi Park
- Summerfield Zoo, Belvidere
- Volcano Falls
- Winnebago County Fairgrounds
- YMCA of Rock River Valley

Galena, IL
Poopsie's and Spotsie's

Chicago, IL

- Art Institute of Chicago
- Field Museum
- Millennium Park
- Museum of Science and Industry
- Navy Pier
- Shedd Aquarium

School Districts and Programs: Grandparent Days

- Classical Conversations: Home School
- Genoa/Kingston School District #424
- Kinnikinnick Community School District #131
- McClain County Normal, IL School District #5
- Rockford Christian School

Cityscape by Faith, at 6

Acknowledgments

After five years working with my family, friends, and colleagues, it is difficult to know where to begin and how to express the gratitude for all who have supported this unique journey and who have made such a positive impact on my life.

Let me begin with my beloved AATH (Association for Applied and Therapeutic Humor) family who continue to support my work. Special thanks go to my fellow Humor Academy directors—Nila Nielsen and Karyn Buxman, along with key advisor Sporty King. Thanks to Barb Best, Ros Ben-Moche, Deb Gauldin, Roberta Gold, Barbara Grapstein, Jana Greco-Crawford, Harald Ellingsen, David Jacobson, Jennifer Keith, Kathy Laurenhue, Melissa Mork, Don and Alleen Nilsen, Jae Pierce-Baba, Katherine Puckett, Bron Roberts, Angie Robinson with a huge thanks to Danny Donuts-Raudonis of Otter Time Productions.

Grateful for the story and quote contributions from Jan Bowman, Kathy Brown, Jan and Bob Jakeway, Jill Knox, Mary Royer, Joyce Saltman, Jean Smith, and Amy Wasil.

My previous work family contributed to my first two books and continue to share their support. Thanks Marcy Mitchell, Lori Fanello, Jack and Sue Finlan, and Jan Bowman, with fond memories of Dr. Richard Fairgrieves and Jeanne Wyatt.

My local support community includes my Seedlings Garden friends and my colleagues in Rockford Network for Women. Kudos to the YMCA staff and workout family who inspire me to stay in shape with a special thanks to instructor Jennifer Drager-Smith.

For all who have invited me to present workshops—you are a blessing! I have lost track over 35 years, but I have been invited to speak to thousands of groups on the benefits of play and humor. I am always energized by the contributions of participants.

Grateful for the incredible testimonials for this book from Dr. Michael Miller, Dr. Earl Henslin, Willibald Ruch, Marilee Sprenger, Brenda Elsagher, Chip Lutz, Kathy Klaus, Debra Hart, Deb Price, Kathy Brown, Don and Alleen Nilsen, Laurie Young, and Peter Jonas.

Thank you to the patient preview editors including Barb Best, Karen Lang, Brenda Elsagher, Kathy Brown, and Bev Letcher. Grateful for an amazing marketing support team including Kristin Oakley, Gina Barreca, Mary Couzin, Heather Greenwood Davis, Allen Klein, Amanda Ferris, Tom Guetzke, Chip Lutz, Heather Walker, Stacy Wallace, Michele St. Clair, with special gratitude to my dear friend Kathy Velasco.

Thanks to my wonderful friend Kyle Edgell for incredible graphic design work including making sure every bubble was correctly placed on the cover and for amazing creative designs for the Playbook! Thanks for the assistance from John Kitchen.

What can I say about an incredible editor, Deb McKew, who saw my vision for this book before I could imagine it and did a remarkable job with the layout and design? You brought this book to life with your experience and creativity. You are a blessing for all who will be reading this book. I will be forever grateful for your expertise and for the fun of working with you.

I want to give a huge shout-out to the Duncan and Wiltz families including my siblings and countless cousins. A special thanks to my brothers, Richard and Steve Wiltz, for their contributions. We are blessed with three living aunts in their 90s: Rosemary Duncan, Rosemary Wiltz, and Florence Duncan. Thanks to Jennifer and Beth Morrison for their support. If all my relatives buy a book—it will be a best seller!

A huge THANK YOU to my immediate family who shared quotes, stories, artwork, and advice. Writing a book with a family of 25 might seem an impossible task, I am grateful for their honest opinions, recommendations, and continuous support. This book would not have been possible without them.

Finally, our incredible grandchildren provided the foundation for the legacy of laughter in this book. I am incredibly proud of each of their amazing contributions. My love and endless gratitude go to Ben, Tyler, Andrew, Samuel, Emma, Mimi, Christine, Katie,

Steve, Cloe, Isaiah, and Faith. Their parents deserve just a tiny bit of credit! Your love means everything: William, Jennifer, Andy, Julie, Rachael, Jason, Peter, and Val.

Finally, this book is a tribute to Don, my husband and soulmate, who not only took most of the pictures, but spent hours trying to find the perfect fit for the text, looking through the 20K assortment of 21 years of photos that were stored on our computers. He not only patiently read and reread each word of the manuscript but made me laugh when my eyes were glazed over from the endless bullet points that seemed to have a habit of jumping off the page. I am grateful he is a REAL swinger too, as we enjoy countless hours of swinging in our yard. This book just would not have happened without his love and support.

Katie, at 14

163

CPSIA information can be obtained
at www.ICGtesting.com
Printed in the USA
LVHW070805020323
740629LV00001B/1